Images of
My Self

Jean Gill

Images of My Self

Meditation and
Self Exploration
Through the Jungian
Imagery of
the Gospels

PAULIST PRESS
New York/Ramsey

Library of Congress
Catalog Card Number: 82-81188

ISBN: 0-8091-2463-7

Published by Paulist Press
545 Island Road, Ramsey, N.J. 07446

Printed and bound in the
United States of America

CONTENTS

Dedicated to
my parents
who are images for me
of God's constant and unconditional love

INTRODUCTION

In the process of giving presentations and leading various prayer experiences, I have met many hungry and thirsty people. They hunger for a more intimate and nurturing relationship with God. They thirst for a deeper and richer spiritual life. They experience a desire for a more fulfilling prayer life, but also feel a sense of frustration and inadequacy in their attempts to grow in this area. Together we have discovered and begun to tear down barriers to spiritual growth. We have begun to replace the obstacles with a new road and a new map to guide us. I have been gratified to see many go their way with renewed inspiration and confidence. This book is my attempt to share the road map which I have used as a guide on this spiritual journey. The approach to the gospels which I have taken adds a new dimension to the stories which are already familiar to most Christians. It is a dimension which is especially valuable when used in personal reflection and prayer.

In their search for spiritual growth, more and more Christians have turned to Eastern meditation in recent years. For those of you who have done so, it should be an easy step to incorporate the Christian meditation methods described herein. In fact, using the familiar imagery of the gospel stories might remove some difficulties you may have encountered as you attempted to adjust your Western ways to the unfamiliar Eastern philosophy and imagery.

I am convinced that meditation is a way of prayer that is possible for all of us. It is not a special gift possessed by an elite

1

few, but a basic human faculty. It is an ability which many of us have simply not developed, perhaps lacking the motivation or the confidence or the knowledge of how to go about it. This book is offered as a guide . . .

for those who want to begin . . .
for those who have tried and failed . . .
for those who already use meditation
and would welcome a fresh approach
through Christian imagery . . .
and for those who may not necessarily want to practice
meditation, but who desire a growth in self-awareness
and a more intimate knowledge
of our Lord Jesus Christ,
who calls us to become fully human and whole . . .
and who is for us an image and model
of that fullness and that wholeness.
I invite you to journey with me to the depths of your being . . .
to find yourself reflected in the images of the gospels . . .
and to walk hand-in-hand with the Lord
toward becoming all that you can be
at each moment of your life.

Acknowledgments

I am grateful first of all to those who have participated in my workshops, prayed with me and shared their experiences. It was with and through them that my ideas were tried and brought to life.

Special thanks are due to Father Joseph Caldwell, S.J. of the Jesuit Retreat House at Los Altos, California, who reviewed the manuscript from his perspective as spiritual director and psychologist. His comments were particularly significant because of his special interests in Jungian psychology and in the use of imagery in prayer. His affirmation and encouragement gave me the confidence to continue.

I am especially grateful to my family and friends for their enthusiastic support and for giving me so many helpful suggestions. I owe particular thanks to my daughter, Mary Dent, who helped with the final typing. My deepest gratitude goes to my husband Walt for his constant, loving encouragement and his valuable suggestions.

1

WELLS & WELLSPRINGS

Imagine a well . . .
    the old-fashioned kind . . .
        with a little shingled roof,
        and an oaken bucket, hanging from a rope . . .
        and a handle, to raise and lower the bucket.
Look at the well from a distance.
    Imagine the landscape—the setting of the well.
        Slowly . . . leisurely . . . picture the surrounding
            countryside . . . mountains . . . hills . . .
                plains . . .
        the vegetation . . . sparse or lavish . . .
            ordinary or magnificent.
    Notice the season of the year.
        Feel the warmth or coolness of the air.
        Smell the air.
Now draw close to the well.
    Stand beside it and touch it.
    Feel the coolness and strength of the stone sides . . .
        the texture of the wooden parts . . .
        the smoothness of the handle,
        its resistance to being turned . . .

the weight of the bucket, and
the roughness of its wood . . .
the coarseness of the rope, its strength,
its flexibility.
Look into the depths of the well.
Follow the inside of the shaft with your eyes
as far as you can see . . .
to the point where the outer light
can penetrate no further . . .
and there is darkness at the depths . . .
and your eyes cannot see the water.
Feel the coolness rising from the depths.
Smell the freshness of the pure, clear spring water in the well.
And know that you are very like the well.
You have at your depths a wellspring
of clear, cool water . . .
an unlimited source of wisdom . . . creativity . . .
strength . . . goodness . . . power.
You have the ability to draw up
from your innermost depths
that great untapped energy . . .
to bring to the light of your consciousness
your own inner resources . . .
and to drink your fill . . .
to satisfy the thirsting of your parched soul . . .
and to share your rich gift with all those whose
lives you touch . . .
and to sing and dance for joy . . .
to celebrate life in its fullness.
And to know that you have met your God within.

Most of us have heard that we develop only a tiny fraction
of our potential and that it is possible to actualize more and
more of our inner resources. But many of us find ourselves

frustrated repeatedly when we see a glimmer of what we can be, and then fall short of becoming it.

A large part of the problem could be that our bucket-lowering mechanism is in very bad shape. It has fallen into a state of deterioration, the result of long-standing neglect. The slats of our oaken bucket are dried out and shrunken, so that the bucket no longer holds water. If we do occasionally try to dip into the well, all the water runs out before it gets back up to us. The rope is brittle and rotting, likely to break from the weight of the water. The handle will barely turn, so rusty and stiff is the mechanism from exposure and disuse.

A discouraging picture? Not at all! Simple to repair, really. All it takes is:

- the *conviction* that our wellspring is really there at our depths and that it is worth our seeking;
- the *willingness* to roll up our sleeves and begin the simple repairs that are needed;
- even lacking the conviction, an *adventuresome spirit* will do quite nicely, so that we are motivated to invest some time and effort to see if the wellspring might be there!

Let us begin the rejuvenation of . . . *Bucket . . . Rope . . . and Handle.*

The Bucket

The bucket is the container that will hold what is at our unconscious depths while we draw it up to the light of our conscious awareness. At the dark depth of the well is that which is unknown within ourselves—that which we cannot see, of which we are not aware. The part of ourselves that is conscious is the part of the well above ground, where the light is able to reach and we are able to see.

The bucket is our capacity for imagery. Work with dreams

has led psychiatrists to discover that our unconscious self prefers a language of symbols and images. If we wish to establish closer communication with our inner depths—to discover and bring to light the great potential that resides there—then we must learn the language of imagery. We already know that language to a greater or lesser degree; but largely because of our scientific, rational, physically-oriented Western culture, many of us have allowed our capacity for symbols and imagery to diminish through disuse. Our culture has tended to minimize the importance of inner, spiritual reality, even to look upon it with suspicion or simply pretend it does not exist. We have allowed the wood of our "imagery bucket" to dry out and shrink, so that the bucket no longer holds water; we lose the messages from our depths before they reach the light of our consciousness. Now we must remedy the situation if we are to make any great headway in communicating with our inner self.

Last summer, my husband bought a half-barrel made of wooden slats held together by metal bands. He thought it would be a great thing to use for keeping beer and soft drinks cool for a backyard party. When he brought it home and I saw it, I couldn't imagine how it would ever hold the ice water. It looked as if it would leak badly. I suggested we give up the idea and put a plant in it instead. But he was not so easily daunted. He knew more about wooden barrels than I. He filled it with water, watched the water stream out between the slats, and refilled it. This process continued until the lower half really did begin to hold the water. He let it sit overnight and refilled it the next day. By the end of the day he could fill it to the top and it held the water! The wood had absorbed the water and had swollen enough to form watertight seams between the slats. My husband had rejuvenated the wooden barrel so that it could again hold water, and I discovered the ways of the natural wooden container.

If the wooden bucket is our capacity for imagery, then the way to repair it is to saturate it with images—or to deliberately practice perceiving and forming images and symbols. In short, we need to practice using our imagination—"thinking with our hearts" instead of mainly with our heads.

There is nothing against logical, rational, "head-thinking." The point is that we're out of balance toward the side of rational thinking. We know quite well how to do that, and we don't need to deliberately practice an ability we already possess and, in fact, exercise constantly. "Head-thinking" will take care of itself. We need to concentrate on "heart-thinking" to bring ourselves into balance, so that both ways of perceiving reality can function with ease.

Throughout this book we will explore techniques for repairing our buckets which can help us to revive our ability to think with our hearts in imagery and symbolism. One good way to begin practicing is to try to look at the everyday things of nature in a symbolic way, as opposed to a rational way. For example, look at a tree. Experience the tree with all of your physical senses. See it in detail. Observe the general shape, the texture of the bark and the leaves. Hear the wind through its branches. Touch it. Smell it. Avoid the urge to think rationally about the biological wonders of the tree. Set aside for the moment such considerations as the process of photosynthesis in the leaves, or the capillary action of the roots. In addition to using your physical senses, use your emotions. Try to feel like a tree. Imagine how it would feel to lose your leaves in winter and "come back to life" in spring, to reach deep into the ground with your roots, drawing up water and nutrients from the earth. Use a similar technique with anything in nature—a rock, a spider, the surf, a brook, a flower. The same thing can be done with man-made and artificial things in the environment, but if our bucket is very dried out, nature seems to be an easier first step. There is something about the images of nature that seems to resonate more easily with the depths of our unconscious. But if you find yourself feeling like a motorcycle, go with it! Let that image speak to you. We need to learn to hear the nudgings of our intuitions, for they may have a message of great value from our inner self.

One exercise you might do right now is to go back to the well symbol with which we began this chapter. Go through it very slowly and deliberately again. If you come to something in the surrounding countryside or the well itself that seems to resonate with you, stop and experience it in as much detail as possible. You might imagine the setting for different seasons of the year, or change the location entirely—maybe from a midwestern countryside to an Arizona desert, or a barren central plain, or a rugged mountain terrain. Use your imagination!

The Rope

The rope is our link between the conscious and the unconscious, between outer and inner reality. A strong rope keeps our bucket from falling and being lost in the darkness of our inner depths. It enables the bucket to be lifted up again and again and brought to the light of consciousness. It helps us maintain that essential balance between outer and inner reality. *The rope is the image we use in making contact with our inner depths.* We can rejuvenate our rotting and weakened rope with images that resonate deeply in the human psyche and are at the same time grounded in solid outer experience. Such images abound in the gospels of Jesus Christ. They can be a sure guide into our inner depths, shedding light where there is darkness. They can be a strong link whereby our inner resources can be drawn out and made manifest in our outer lives. This is one of the deepest experiences of the incarnation—divinity enfleshed—our God within made manifest in our human actions.

There are other sources of these universal images, including the scriptures of other religions and the great myths. However, this book will be limited to the Christian scriptures. In the remaining chapters we will explore specific passages from the gospels, seeking ways they can be used to plumb our inner depths.

It is important to make some distinctions at this point. We can approach the gospels at different levels of meaning, all valid and all important. There is an historical level, which seeks to answer such questions as, "What really happened?" "What does it mean based on the culture and the audience of the writer?" "What was the intent of the writer?" This is the area of scriptural exegesis, and is a valuable basis for the other levels of meaning. We can consider the meaning of a passage in regard to outer reality, or behavior, and also in regard to inner reality. We will be concerned primarily with the inner reality meaning of the gospel passages, considering scriptural exegesis as it is applicable.

Actually, one reason our rope may be stiff and frayed is that many of us have had a limited approach to the gospels—the historical, outer approach. But this is only a part of human perception. We need to strengthen our rope and bring our perception of the gospels to fullness by now including their inner meaning.

The Handle

Having attended to our bucket and our rope, we must also be able to operate the handle mechanism in order to make the contact we seek with our inner depths. *The handle symbolizes a specific technique to set the whole process in motion, and that technique is meditation.* As with bucket and rope, most of us need to repair our handle, which may be quite stiff and rusty from lack of use. To repair it, we need simply to practice the techniques of meditation.

Meditation is a word that has varied meanings, so I will describe what I mean by it. Meditation is not reading nor rational thinking, nor is it an emotional experience—though these can be a valuable prelude to meditation. Meditation is a state of inner quiet in which we set aside the rational, the activities of our daily lives, our thinking activity. We enter another level of awareness in which we communicate with our inner self. Meditation does involve images—not only of sight, but also of smell, touch, sound and taste. It can involve insights and a sense of presence. In other words, *meditation is an experience of com-*

*municating with our inner self in the language of the uncon-
scious: imagery and symbolism.*

Meditation is a deliberate dipping down into the inner
depths of ourselves . . .
in order to draw up to the light of our conscious awareness
some of our inner potential . . .
to drink deeply of its life-giving waters . . .
and hence to go forth into our outer life,
> refreshed and rejuvenated,
> with clearer vision,
> increased creativity,
> greater love for life as we find it,
> further enabled to share our gifts with those
> > whose lives we touch,
allowing our God within to shine forth as light and life and
> love.

And so to begin . . . we need a practical *handle-repairing
guide*—TECHNIQUES FOR PRACTICING MEDITATION.
Following are some suggestions.

1. *Preparation.* The following can be helpful as preparation for meditation:
   a. *reading* something inspirational, such as a scripture
      passage;
   b. *reflecting* on a reading or an experience of your life;
   c. *identifying a present strong emotion*—one that you
      are experiencing at the moment, or that arises again
      when you remember a past experience;
   d. *choosing an image*—perhaps a picture, a place out-
      doors or even an item such as a rock or a flower, to
      use as material for meditation. Music can be very
      helpful in stimulating images within ourselves. The
      choice of music depends on individual taste. Each

person needs to experiment and find what works best for him or her.

2. *Beginning.* There are several important conditions to consider when you are ready to meditate:

    a. *Location*—You'll need a place where you can be alone and undisturbed, preferably a special place, one that is not usually used by you for working or sleeping.

    b. *Position*—Find a position in which you are comfortable but alert. Many find that sitting in a straight-backed chair with both feet on the floor, or sitting on the floor with legs crossed and back straight, works well. The floor position may be worth considering seriously, even if it is uncomfortable at first. There is a closeness to the earth that seems to stimulate our contact with inner reality much the same way that nature images do.

    The position of the hands is worth some attention. If our hands are open, with palms facing upward, we tend to feel more open and vulnerable. This position during meditation can help us achieve an attitude of openness—a sensitivity to the presence of God deep within ourselves.

    c. *Time*—For many of us, this is the catch! But we simply cannot put our handle in good working condition and keep it that way without *regular practice.* For most of us, that means setting aside a *specific time of fifteen to thirty minutes each day,* at least four or five days a week. This is the price we pay. And we need strong motivation to stick with it. We need to be convinced of its value enough to invest the time, taking the risk that the investment will pay off in the long run. The time we set aside deserves to be *prime time*—not a time, for instance, when we are exhausted from the day's work. We need to find a time when we are at our best. Each individual must use his/her ingenuity to find that time in the daily schedule, and perhaps rearrange the schedule to fit it in. To summarize, the conditions of time most conducive to practicing meditation are:

(1) regular practice,
(2) a specific time of the day,
(3) fifteen to thirty minutes in length,
(4) prime time.

One suggestion that may be helpful is to set a wind-up timer for the length of time you want to spend in meditation. Then you need not be distracted by worrying that you'll spend more time than you can afford or that you'll fall asleep and miss an appointment. An electric timer is not as good, because you need to get up and turn it off. A manual timer just rings briefly and stops. Then you can come out of your meditation slowly and gently, or continue a while if you choose.

d. *Silence*—This means not only outer silence but also quieting the thinking and inner conversation that seems constantly to be going on in our minds. This is one of the most difficult conditions to achieve, but also one of the most essential. Unless we can let go of outer reality for this brief time, we will seldom find the way to inner reality. This takes practice, but be patient with yourself and be gentle. Some specific ways to achieve inner silence are:

(1) *Deep breathing*—Slowly, gently, breathe deeply several times. Place your hand on your abdomen just below your ribs. Gently expand your abdomen as you inhale and contract it as you exhale,

until you get the feel of it. This kind of breathing is very helpful in calming our busy minds and relaxing our tense bodies.

(2) *Listen* intently to all the sounds around you. Hear them as signs of God's presence in all of life, especially here, now, with you.

(3) *Feel* the air, your clothes, the chair or floor supporting you. Feel God's presence, surrounding you with love and supporting you with care.

(4) A *mantra* is sometimes helpful. This is a simple word or syllables to say, aloud or in silence, in rhythm with your breathing. Two common mantras are: "Ab-ba" (Jesus' term for the Father, an intimate term like "Daddy" or "Papa"), and "Jesus, Lord."

(5) *Distractions* seem to be a problem for most of us, especially those seemingly constant mental conversations we carry on, which intrude on our attempts at meditation. Some suggestions for dealing with them are:

- *Take the phone off the hook!*
- *Close your eyes.* This eliminates the outer visual distractions of the moment.
- *Gently and patiently set aside the thoughts as they appear,* with a remark such as, "Not now. I'll deal with this later."
- *Jot down briefly* any good ideas that occur, or things you want to remember. Fear of forgetting can make it almost impossible to quiet your thinking. It is good practice to have paper and pencil handy for this purpose.
- *Strong feelings* of the moment cannot easily be set aside. Not only that, but a disturbing emotion such as anger, fear, sorrow or guilt can be an outer

manifestation of something from our inner depths that we have not yet resolved. It can be extremely valuable to incorporate such an emotion into the meditation. "Put a face on it," i.e., imagine what it would look like as a person or creature. For example, a feeling of anger might be imagined as a Nordic warrior figure with ferocious countenance and sword unsheathed. Or jealousy might be depicted as a green, slithering mythical creature with frowning face and beady, squinting eyes. Talk with your emotion-image and try to befriend it.

The above techniques can be helpful in practicing meditation, but no amount of technique will be effective without a strong desire to make meditation a regular part of our life for the purpose of coming to greater self-knowledge and becoming all that we can be. Another attitude that is essential to meditation is that of total openness. I have given up the practice of meditation several times in the past, mainly because my experience of it did not match my expectations. I had hoped for a deep spiritual experience, or at least a feeling of closeness to God. Now I expect nothing. I am willing to spend the time I allot for meditation in simply being open and receptive to the Spirit within. Having any set expectations seems to have been a barrier to even the very experience that I had expected! Only when I was able to let go of my own expectations was I able to use meditation effectively.

It is important to realize that once we open ourselves to the inner, spiritual realm, we open ourselves to a world that can be frightening. However, we need not be fearful if we approach our inner world with the motive of spiritual growth. We have the assurance of Christ that he will be with us and guide us, and we need only call on him. To have a frightening experience can be very worthwhile; in fact it can be a point of great spiritual development. We can be impeded in our growth if we allow our fear to block out such an experience.

We will consider some examples of this later, as we explore specific scriptural passages.

It is important to consider one caution about meditation. The practice of meditation could be dangerous for a person who is seriously unbalanced mentally or emotionally. Such a person may lose the distinction between the inner, spiritual realm and the outer, physical world. He or she could, symbolically, "fall into the well." Our purpose is to draw up the water with both feet planted firmly on the ground of ordinary, everyday, outer living. An unbalanced person could be in danger of being swallowed up in the imagery of the inner world and lose contact with outer reality. Such a person should therefore be discouraged from using meditation.

Let us consider for a moment a topic that is related to meditation: *dreams.* Our unconscious self attempts to communicate with our conscious self through the imagery of our dreams during sleep. It is as though dreams and meditation reach out to communicate from two opposite directions. Dreams reach up toward our conscious self from our unconscious inner depths. In meditation we consciously reach down to contact our inner unconscious self. The two approaches can be quite complementary. If we pay attention to our dreams and attempt to find meaning in them, our ability to meditate seems to grow. Likewise if we are practicing meditation, we seem to be able to remember and understand our dreams more easily. Since both processes deal with the imagery of inner reality, one tends to enhance the other. So as we attempt to grow in our meditation skills, it can be helpful to pay serious attention to our dreams. One useful, easy-to-read book on the understanding of dreams is *The Dream Game* by Ann Faraday (Perennial Library, Harper and Row). The author has made an intriguing observation: as we pay increasingly more attention to dreams, we become more and more able to enter them consciously. We become aware while dreaming that we are dreaming. From the other side, as one practices conscious meditation, the imagery arising spontaneously from the unconscious becomes more and more frequent. From either direction, i.e., from meditation or from dreams, it seems that in time a person is able to open the door between the conscious and the unconscious with increasing ease. That is a most important door for humankind to be able to open. It can be the prelude to the opening of many other doors which separate human beings from each other, and which cause us to look upon each other with fear, suspicion, and ignorance. Open doors lead to truth, trust and unity, within ourselves as well as between ourselves and others.

Let us begin now to saturate our wooden bucket so it will hold water; strengthen and rejuvenate our rope so it will wind and unwind freely and be able to bear the weight of our full bucket; oil our handle and turn it with ease, so that the whole process can be set in motion. I invite you to try the following exercise in meditation.

This will be an exercise in the techniques of meditation, as well as a renewal of our acquaintance with that person who is the main figure of our imagery within the scope of this book: Jesus Christ of the gospels.

Go now to your special meditation place, where you won't be disturbed. Take the phone off the hook and set a timer for fifteen or twenty minutes if you think that will help. Get into a comfortable, alert position, with hands open and palms facing upward if you wish.

Now relax and close your eyes. Breathe deeply into your abdomen a few times, slowly and gently. Listen to all the sounds around you. Cherish them as signs of the presence of God. Feel the air, the weight of your clothes, the pressure of the chair or the floor. Feel the surrounding and supporting love and care of God.

Gently but firmly push aside any thoughts or worries from your life. Write down any that persist, promising that you will attend to them later.

In the gospel of Mark, 6:31, Jesus says to his friends, "Come away by yourselves to a lonely place, and rest a while"

(Revised Standard Version). Let us go away for a little while now, and be with Jesus.

Imagine a place you'd like to go . . .
>   one of your favorite places, perhaps.
> Go there, in your imagination.
> You are alone.
Imagine the scene in as much detail as you can.
> Look at it . . . all of it . . . in detail.
> Hear the sounds.
> Touch the things nearby.
> Smell the air . . . taste it.
> Be still for a few moments.
Then see a man walking toward you from a distance. It is Jesus.
> As he draws near, notice what he looks like.
> How is he dressed?
> >   In contemporary clothing?
> >   In traditional biblical garb?
> Is he bearded or clean-shaven?
Greet him in whatever way you wish as he comes near you.
Spend your time with Jesus in whatever way you wish.
When your meditation period is over, bid goodbye to Jesus,
> until you meet again.
Watch him as he walks away in the same direction from which
> he came.
See him disappear in the distance.

Slowly open your eyes, and gently return to your outer world. Allow your experience to accompany you during the day. Let it grow in meaning as your reflect upon it through your everyday life. Be continually refreshed and nourished by it, and share its cool water with others.

2

AN ADULTERESS & A PHARISEE

There are various ways to use the image materials we choose for meditation. Once we have achieved a state of inner silence, and have chosen an image, we have opened the door to our unconscious inner self. We can open the door and consciously invite our inner self to communicate with us, but we cannot force such communication. It is desirable to cultivate an attitude that we do not expect anything during our time of meditation. If our inner self chooses to communicate, we can receive the gift with open arms, cherish and rejoice in it. If there seems to be no gift on a particular occasion, and we have not expected one, then we are not likely to experience a sense of failure or disappointment. The most cherished gifts are those which are least expected, and that is surely true of our inner surprises!

Let us consider several types of image materials and ways they can be used:

1. *Spontaneous imagery*—We can enter meditation with no image consciously chosen, but rather we try to clear our minds and invite our inner self to present an image. If a spontaneous image appears, we can watch it move and change, and we can also enter into it consciously and direct it. This is a very

active interaction between our inner and outer selves. It can be very meaningful, since our inner self is quite likely to present something that is important for us to notice, but that we may have missed in our conscious life. This is close to the dreaming process.

2. *Still imagery*—We can consciously choose a still image (perhaps a painting or photo) to begin our meditation and wait for it to move spontaneously, guided by our unconscious. If nothing happens, we can start some action consciously and often some spontaneous imagery will follow.

3. *Action/dialogue imagery*—We can choose a story or dialogue with which to begin, and then stop at a certain point. Here we can ask a question of one of the characters or express an emotion, and wait for our inner self to answer through the character. Writing out the dialogue can be very helpful. Or rather than instigating a conversation, we can simply let the action unfold. This is similar to the second way of using images, except that we have already started the action before we begin meditation. This action/dialogue type of imagery is especially useful with many gospel passages. It is the primary approach we will take with the gospel selections in this book.

4. *Guided imagery*—We can choose a written or recorded guided meditation. In this type, we allow someone else to guide the flow of imagery through the meditation. If it is in written form, we read at our own pace and stop where we wish, to let the images develop freely. This type of imagery, being more structured, has less chance of resonating with our own individual inner processes. On the other hand, it has two distinct advantages. Guided imagery can provide inspiration when our "imagery bucket" seems dried out. It can also be effective in holding our attention when we are troubled with distractions. We will use some guided meditations based on the gospel passages to be presented.

Now let us enter into the events and stories of the gospels together, to seek their inner meaning, and to hear the message of Christ spoken from the depths of our being. We will follow a general four-step procedure in approaching each passage.

Step 1: *Scriptural Background*—a brief presentation of any scholarly background that seems pertinent to the inner meaning of the passage.

Step 2: *Re-creating the event* as if we were there, mainly by considering the feelings and motives of the characters.

Step 3: A consideration of the possible *inner meaning* of the event—mainly by asking ourselves such questions as, "Who is my inner paralytic or blind person? my inner adulteress or Pharisee? my inner widow?" and "What is the voice of Christ within me? What do I hear him say to me?"

Step 4: The *actual meditation.*

The first passage we will consider is from the gospel according to John (8:1–11), the story of the woman caught in adultery:

They went each to his own house, but Jesus went to the Mount of Olives. Early in the morning he came again to the temple; all the people came to him, and he sat down and taught them. The scribes and Pharisees brought a woman who had been caught in the act of adultery, and placing her in the midst they said to him, "Teacher, this woman has been caught in the act of adultery. Now in the law Moses commanded us to stone such. What do you say about her?" This they said to test him, that they might have some charge to bring against him. Jesus bent down and wrote with his finger on the ground. And as they continued to ask him, he stood up and said to them, "Let him who is without sin among you be the first to throw a stone at her." And once more he bent down and wrote with his finger on the ground. But when they heard it, they went away, one by one, beginning with the eldest, and Jesus was left alone with the woman standing before him. Jesus looked up and said to her, "Woman, where are they? Has no one condemned you?" She said, "No one, Lord." And Jesus said, "Neither do I condemn you; go, and do not sin again." (Revised Standard Version)

Step 1—Scriptural Background

Based on the situation of the time, the scribes and Pharisees probably hope to trap Jesus in a dilemma: if he agrees with the sentence, the Romans could charge him with inciting the others to kill the woman; if he disagrees with the sentence, the Jews could charge him with condoning the sin of the woman.

Jesus' reference to "him who is without sin" refers to sin in general, and does not imply that the accusers were adulterers.

The word "condemn" in this text means to pass sentence. Hence Jesus' refusal to condemn her does not imply that he condones the action of the woman, but rather that he does not agree with carrying out the harsh sentence of death.

As for the writing on the ground, the meaning is unclear.

Step 2—Re-creating the Event

Try to visualize the scene of the accusation. Jesus is teaching the people, who are gathered around him. The scribes and Pharisees bring the woman into the midst of the group and pose their question to Jesus.

What feelings do you think the woman is experiencing? Fear? A sense of worthlessness? Hopelessness? Guilt? Anger? Resentment? How do you think she feels while Jesus is writing, and as her accusers turn away? Bewilderment? Anxiety? A ray of hope? How about her feelings when Jesus refuses to condemn her and then sets her free? Relief? Disbelief? Elation? A sense of self-worth returning? Anxiety about what lies ahead? Confusion? Gratitude? Hope?

Consider the scribes and Pharisees. How do you think they feel as they bring the woman before Jesus and the crowd? Superior? Self-righteous? Confident? Powerful? Jealous? How do they feel during Jesus' response? Frustrated? Angry? Threatened? Confused? Embarrassed? Losing control?

It is important to consider Jesus' attitude toward the woman as it is implied in the text, and as contrasted with the attitude of the scribes and Pharisees. First of all, he clearly sees the woman's life as having a higher value than the strict adherence to the law indicates. He also apparently considers it important to point out to her that there is a positive direction in which she can grow. While he lets her know that she has been involved in a destructive relationship ("do not sin again"), he also urges her to move on, with the simple command to "go." It is as though he were to say, "You've made a mistake. Learn from it. Avoid repeating it. You are too worthwhile and valuable a person to remain in this destructive relationship. Rise up out of it. Leave it behind. Move on to something greater, in which you can bring to fruition the potential that I can see in you."

Step 3—Inner Meaning

As a general guideline, one of the most direct ways to find the inner meaning of a passage for yourself is to focus on the emotions of the characters and identify the same feelings in your own inner dialogue. Looking back at the various emotions you think the adulteress was experiencing during the unfolding of the story, you can probably identify those same feelings in yourself within your own personal experience. You can probably do the same in considering the feelings of the group of scribes and Pharisees. (For the sake of simplicity, we will consider the group of scribes and Pharisees as a single personality, referred to simply as the Pharisee.) Now consider the dialogue that takes place within yourself sometimes that seems very familiar when you observe the relationship between the adulteress and the Pharisee, especially in the context of the feelings you identified. *Most of us can recognize that we have an inner adulteress and an inner Pharisee who are sometimes engaged in a similar interchange.*

25

Consider the basic roles of the main figures in the scene. The *adulteress:*

- is accused of an act of infidelity.
- is brought before Jesus for judgment.

The *Pharisee:*

- accuses the adulteress of infidelity.
- brings the adulteress before Jesus.
- proposes condemnation (death by stoning).
- attempts to trap Jesus.

Jesus is the *guide,* the one who *clarifies the issues,* as he:

- accepts the accusation ("Do not sin again").
- rejects the condemnation ("Neither do I condemn you").
- eludes the trap.
- calls the adulteress to growth beyond her present sin of infidelity ("Go. . .").

What is this sin which the Pharisee brings to light? It is a sin of adultery—infidelity to the true spouse or betrothed. From the viewpoint of inner meaning, it can be viewed as an infidelity to our true self—who we are and who we can become. In this context, our inner Pharisee is a valuable part of our self. It is he who brings to light our infidelity and brings us before Jesus so that we are able to hear his words of forgiveness and encouragement, his call to become all that we can be. While the Pharisee is a valuable "inner self" for us, *it is very important to know when to stop listening to our Pharisee and to start listening to Jesus. That point is when the Pharisee condemns us. We must let the Pharisee leave then and we must stay with Jesus to draw from his healing strength.* For if we accept our Pharisee's condemnation and agree that we are

26

worthless, we will be unable to hear those healing words of unconditional love spoken by Jesus, and we will be unable to move on. In effect, we will allow the Pharisee to trap Jesus!

In the imagery of this gospel passage we see played out before us a basic pattern of human growth which is repeated many times over within each of us as we strive to become all that we can be. There is first of all an awareness of dissatisfaction and discomfort. We become conscious that some attitude or characteristic action of ours is somehow not the best that is in us. We see an infidelity to our true self that we had not seen before. Second, we often resist this call to change. We react to our new consciousness with a variety of emotions, all the way from anxiety and fear to anger or guilt, and, finally and hopefully, to acceptance. This brings us, third, to the realization or the call to growth, the hope of new beginnings. Fourth, we are empowered to rise up and move on, to take on a new attitude that is more faithful to our true self.

Meditation using the imagery of this gospel passage can be a source of great power and wisdom in the progressive unfolding of our true selves. It can help keep us from getting stuck midway through the process, help us move through to real growth. *Where reasoning and "will power" often fail to help us change, the language of imagery can enable us to accomplish the growth we desire.*

Within the basic framework of the story of the adulteress, there is a lot of open space for us to fill in between the lines. This is where our disturbing emotions are especially valuable. They can point the way to a specific attitude or experience which contains the seeds of growth at a particular time; they get our attention by causing us discomfort. We can incorporate these emotions into the adulteress story as it unfolds, and often find a valuable insight or motivation for growth in that particular area. We make the story our own by incorporating into it our feelings and experience. We color the imagery with our emotions—and end up with distinctively different stories while remaining within the basic framework.

Perhaps a couple of examples from my own experience will help to clarify this. Several years ago I decided to try to improve my communications with others, especially with my husband and children. I had read and heard of new concepts of interpersonal communications, especially of the value of identifying and expressing feelings, and of hearing the feelings behind the words spoken by others. Deeply convinced of the value of this new approach, I consciously tried to put into practice what I had learned. I was alternately encouraged by my successes and discouraged by my failures. It was difficult to undo the habits of a lifetime. One day after about a year of effort, it seemed to me that my failures far outnumbered my successes. I thought that by then I should have been able to change my habits. I began to feel more and more depressed. All the successes seemed to count for nothing. I had wanted to learn this way of communicating more fully and lovingly, and it seemed I had failed utterly. I felt totally worthless. I stopped short at that point and realized I could not believe that I really was no good. I recalled a statement I had heard before and believed: "God does not make junk." This was the turning point. I began to emerge from my sense of worthlessness and move toward a more balanced perspective. I still recall this experience vividly. It was an important point in my life. I not only regained my self-esteem, but came to a more realistic and patient view of my own growth process.

Based on this experience, the imagery of the passage could be colored by my emotions to appear something like the following:

My inner adulteress is caught in an act of infidelity to my self, in failing to say what I really felt or hear what others really said. My feelings of worthlessness and guilt could be expressed by her clothing—a dirty gray hooded cloak—and by her slouching posture, with head hanging in shame and eyes cast down.

My inner Pharisee is a merciless accuser, proclaiming the worthlessness of my adulteress by condemning her to death. His attitude of scathing condemnation could be expressed in his face, contorted in ugly hatred and self-righteousness, and in his voice, screaming degrading names at her.

The turning point of my experience could be expressed in the moment when my adulteress hears Jesus' call to learn from her mistake and to move on to become more truly the person of value that he sees her to be. In the imagery of the passage, my recovered self-esteem and realistic acceptance of my process of growth could be expressed in the figure of the adulteress now standing tall, head held high, discarding the gray cloak and moving on.

Let us consider a different experience, and see how it colors the basic adulteress story differently. A couple of years ago, a person came into my life whom I grew to dislike intensely. I found myself in one conflict after another with the person. My resentment, anger, frustration and guilt grew with each conflict. I could not succeed in changing myself and I knew it was counter-productive to attempt to change another person, though I found myself repeatedly wishing for that. A good friend told me that what we dislike in another person is likely to be something that we have failed to recognize and accept in ourself. I considered her comment seriously, but could not find anything in the person that I thought was like me. It took over a year for me to finally decide that she must be right, since nothing else had worked to resolve the situation. Then I took a more serious look. I found immediately what that quality was—a desire to be possessively in control, expressed in feelings of jealousy and anger. It was a great relief and another turning point. I had taken a concrete step toward empathy with the other person, and it was the beginning of a positive growth in self-knowledge for me.

With this experience in mind, the imagery of the passage could be colored something like this:

> My inner adulteress is accused by my Pharisee of infidelity. In contrast to the adulteress of the first example, my adulteress now is belligerent and resentful. She will not accept the accusation of the Pharisee and tells him in no uncertain terms what he can do with his stupid laws! Her belligerence is an image of my inability to see my own negative quality.

> My inner Pharisee, again in contrast to the first example, calmly and matter-of-factly repeats the accusation and tells her that she will have to come with him for sentencing. His attitude is an image of the persistence with which my friend's statement repeatedly recurred to me before I finally accepted it.

> My Pharisee brings the adulteress before Jesus. It is only through Jesus' statement of her personal value that she is finally able to accept the fact of her infidelity—failing to acknowledge and relate to that part of my true self that wants to be in possessive control. This turning point in my self-knowledge is expressed in the face and stance of the adulteress. Her resentment falls aways, and her face looks calm and hopeful. She turns and moves away confidently, accepting Jesus' challenge to become all that she can be. This expresses my acceptance of that part of myself that likes to be in control and my search for ways to use that quality in positive ways.

Step 4—Meditation

Having considered the passage as though it were being enacted on a stage in front of us, let us step into the scene in meditation and imagine the characters as parts of our inner self. Watch the scene unfold and speak to you.

Begin by taking time to quiet down and make yourself open to your inner depths. Follow the preparation suggestions in Chapter 1 that are helpful to you.

Then simply allow the scene to unfold. Set the mood according to your own feelings and experience. See the adulteress and the Pharisee as parts of your self. Move the action forward consciously if you want, but let it occur spontaneously and go with it if that happens. It will often be a combination of both. Let it proceed past the end of the gospel passage if you feel so inclined. It is possible that your meditation will become too painful or frightening and that you will not feel strong enough to let it go on. If this happens you can simply decide to stop. Or, remembering that Jesus is there with you, you may decide to see it through with him to guide and protect you.

It can be extremely fruitful to return to this passage occasionally as a basis for meditation. Since it is an image of a basic human growth process, its repeated use can help you to move through that process as it occurs within different experiences in your life. It can be a powerful image to help us avoid getting stuck with the Pharisee, either in blindness to a part of our true self or in a paralyzing sense of worthlessness proclaimed by his condemnation. We need to hear Jesus' call repeatedly, as we come to know more clearly who we are and who we can become. We need to see his hand outstretched to us in encouragement to move on and to grow ever more faithful to our true selves.

3

A CHILD & A FATHER

Let us consider the story of the raising of the daughter of Jairus, Mark 5:21–24,35–43 (Revised Standard Version):

> And when Jesus had crossed again in the boat to the other side, a great crowd gathered about him; and he was beside the sea. Then came one of the rulers of the synagogue, Jairus by name; and seeing him, he fell at his feet, and besought him, saying, "My little daughter is at the point of death. Come and lay your hands on her, so that she may be made well, and live." And he went with him. . . .
>
> While he was still speaking, there came from the ruler's house some who said, "Your daughter is dead. Why trouble the Teacher any further?" But ignoring what they said, Jesus said to the ruler of the synagogue, "Do not fear, only believe." And he allowed no one to follow him except Peter and James and John the brother of James. When they came to the house of the ruler of the synagogue, he saw a tumult, and people weeping and wailing loudly. And when he had entered he said to them, "Why do you make a tumult and weep? The child is not dead but sleeping." And they laughed at him. But he put them all outside, and

took the child's father and mother and those who were with him, and went in where the child was. Taking her by the hand he said to her, "Talitha cumi"; which means, "Little girl, I say to you, arise." And immediately the girl got up and walked; for she was twelve years old. And immediately they were overcome with amazement. And he strictly charged them that no one should know this, and told them to give her something to eat.

As before, we will approach the passage in four steps.

Step 1—Scriptural Background

Jairus as a ruler of the synagogue showed an unusual openness. Synagogue officials as a group tended to be traditional and unlikely to be open to the new and the untried. Out of deep concern for his daughter, Jairus was willing to risk the disapproval of his peers to approach this new and unauthorized teacher, Jesus of Nazareth.

Step 2—Re-creating the Event

Try to picture the scene of Jairus' encounter with Jesus. Jesus is by the sea, surrounded by the crowd, when Jairus approaches him with his plea to come and heal his dying little girl.

What emotions do you think Jairus is experiencing? Fear of losing his daughter? Fear of ridicule by his peers? Desperation? How do you think he feels when he is told that his child is dead? Despairing? Grievous? Disbelieving? How about Jairus' feelings when Jesus says, "Do not fear, only believe"? A glimmer of hope returning? Confidence in Jesus? Confusion? What about Jairus' feelings when the mourners laugh at Jesus? Doubtful? Embarrassed? Insecure? Afraid?

Let us consider the child. She is mortally ill, helpless, dependent on her father to seek healing for her. Perhaps she drifts in and out of consciousness as she approaches the edge of death. What might be her feelings? Fear? Loneliness? Bitterness? Despair? Or resignation? Acceptance? Hope? Anticipation? How might she feel when she comes back to life? Surprised? Confused? Ecstatic? Rejuvenated? Strong? Hungry?

How do you think Jairus and the girl's mother feel as she arises and walks? Incredulous? Overjoyed? Awe-struck?

Observe Jesus' actions and words as the passage progresses. Notice his confidence throughout. After agreeing to go with Jairus to heal his daughter, Jesus is unperturbed by the reports that she is already dead. Arriving at Jairus' house, Jesus remains steadfast in the face of ridicule by the crowd of mourners. The passage ends with a concise statement of Jesus' perception of the needs of a child—his simple request that she be given some food.

Step 3—Inner Meaning

In searching for an inner meaning in this passage, it is essential to explore the meaning of the child. She is the central figure of the story. It is her sickness and death which causes her father to seek out Jesus, and which provides Jesus with the opportunity to heal and to give life. It is her return to life that brings the family back to equilibrium and enables them to resume their day-to-day living. While she was sick their whole life was paralyzed in a way, with all their energy focused on caring for her.

Let us consider some of the characteristics of a child. A child is inquisitive . . . sensitive . . . trusting . . . dependent . . . adventurous . . . emotional . . . receptive . . . open . . . creative . . . playful . . . searching . . . mischievous . . . imaginative . . . growing . . . accepting . . . full of wonder and awe . . . curious.

We each have an inner child with characteristics like these. This passage thrusts some urgent questions upon us:

- Is our inner child dead, or dying?
- Do we need to send our inner parent to seek out Jesus, to

beckon him to come and return our child to fullness of life?

- Does our child need nourishment?

To help find some answers, let us focus on four of the traits mentioned above which are especially significant. The first trait is *growth*. A child grows through many stages in developing to maturity. We expect and accept these stages of growth and cherish the child throughout the process. For example, we expect a child who is learning to walk to stumble many times. We know that falling is part of the learning process. We can be there to pick her up and bandage the wounds, but we cannot avoid the falling for her. She must stumble to learn; we do not love her any less, nor do we scold her for stumbling.

Another example is that of a child learning to write. We don't scold him when his first efforts result in illegible scribbles. We know that this is an essential part of the process, and we even save and cherish the scribbles.

Growth does not end with physical maturity. As long as we are alive, we continue to grow. We continually discover new capabilities and resources within ourselves, and we go through stages of learning to use our abilities. We discover new insights and struggle to incorporate them into our daily actions and attitudes. All of this growth, like the physical growth of a child, can be said to be accomplished by our inner child. Our inner child goes through stages of the growth process which seem just as inefficient and frustrating as the growing stages of the physical child. Yet we sometimes scold ourselves unmercifully for all our stumbling and scribbling. We expect instant results. We are perfectionists, unwilling to tolerate the stages of the learning process, satisfied only with the final achievement. A child could be hindered in the normal development of physical skills by undue pressure and scolding during the learning process. Likewise, our inner child becomes stifled and can shrivel and die from our own scolding and unrealistic expectations. We need to learn to cherish our mistakes as normal parts of our growth processes and as opportunities for learning. In that way, we allow our inner child to be touched repeatedly by the healing and life-giving hand of the Lord. Our inner child can arise and walk again and again with wonder and joy.

The trait of *playfulness* is the second one that we will single out for special attention. The work ethic of our Western culture tends to diminish our appreciation of this aspect of our inner child. Pure enjoyment with no practical purpose is often viewed as worthless. Many of us have become more or less "workaholics." We know now that the ability to "let go" and play is essential to human growth. Without it we tend to become stilted, closed, rigid persons. Many of us need to learn again how to play, allowing our inner child to come back to life.

The third trait of the child at which we will look more closely is that of *feeling*, or being *in touch with emotions*. A child tends to respond to experiences on an emotional level, expressing feelings quite freely. The very young child has little control over his or her response to an emotion. As the child grows, control of the response develops, and the child grows in ability to express feelings in constructive ways. The child begins to see some responses as constructive and acceptable, and others as destructive and unacceptable. Unfortunately, in this process many of us became confused in our perception. We confused our emotions with our response to our emotions. We began to view our emotions as good or bad, rather than limiting our judgment to our response to the emotions. As a result, we learned to suppress or deny our "bad" emotions. We became progressively less sensitive to our feelings, even to the point where we could be experiencing anger or fear or hurt, and be almost totally unaware of the emotion. We learned to bury the feelings within ourselves—but we buried them alive and they did not die! Emotions thus denied will express themselves unconsciously as physical or emotional disorders, or in destructive behavior or attitudes.

In burying our feelings we bring a deathly illness upon our

inner child. We lose touch with one of our most valuable guides to growth and wholeness; we decrease our capacity to live life fully. We need to change our perception in order to allow this part of our inner child to be healed. We need to see all of our emotions, not as good or bad, but as expressions of ourselves, as signs of our own unique response to our life experiences. Then we need to cherish those feelings—all of them. It is only when we can consciously feel our emotions that we have control over how we respond to them. The more fully aware we are in experiencing our emotions, the more fully we can live and love and become all that we can be.

As a step toward enabling this emotional part of your inner child to be healed, you might try this exercise:

1. Write down all the emotions you can think of.
2. Accept yourself as being capable of feeling each of them.
3. Cherish each emotion.

If you are unable to find any value in a certain feeling, try to recall a time when you experienced that emotion. Try to see what you learned about yourself through that experience. Cherish it as a step in your growth. If you have trouble thinking of emotions for your list, you might try some of these: afraid, insecure, wishy-washy, angry, jealous, ashamed, foolish, hurt, rejected, betrayed, helpless, dependent, sad, happy, ecstatic, sexy, playful, warm, loving, curious, proud.

The fourth trait of a child on which we will focus is *trust*. This characteristic is closely related to *dependence* and *openness*. The child trusts the parents, is dependent on them and is open to receive the gifts of love and nourishment the parents bestow. These are traits we need to nurture within ourselves. We tend to think of dependency as a sign of weakness, and it can be. As adults, we need to find a balance between dependence and independence. If we try to be totally independent, our inner child will suffer. We need to trust others to a degree and accept their gifts as willingly as a child. Especially we need to trust God completely, to acknowledge our dependence on our Creator, and to open our hands to receive the gifts our Father gives, as well as to allow him to take back some of those gifts. Like a child, we do not always see the gifts as our Father sees them. What we think is good for ourselves, God may not see that way, and vice versa. God our Father is like a caring and responsible human father. There are things a father may give or require of his child that the child does not want; or the father may withhold something the child wants, knowing it is not good for the child at the time. The father is able to understand much that the child cannot, and so it is with God our Father.

Throughout the gospels Jesus demonstrates an attitude of trust and openness toward his Father, expressed especially well in his use of the name *Abba* for his Father. *Abba* is translated as "Daddy" or "Papa," implying an intimate relationship and a greater degree of dependence and trust than the more formal term of Father.

In another part of Mark's gospel (Mark 10:13–16), Jesus states the necessity of being childlike—in that familiar scene in which Jesus gathers the children to himself and blesses them. He states that unless we receive the kingdom of God like a little child we shall not enter it. In the light of the characteristics of a child which we have just considered, this strong statement of Jesus takes on a broader meaning than what we might have understood before.

Now consider these characteristics of a child from your own personal experience—the traits of *growth, playfulness, feeling,* and *trust.* Ponder whether any of those qualities need to be rejuvenated within yourself. Assess the state of health of your inner child.

Can you recognize the gospel scene unfolding within yourself? Perhaps you have decided to try to change an attitude or a habit, but you encounter frequent failures in the process. An inner voice nags, "You should give it up. You can't do it. You should keep the old way anyway; it is easier and safer." Or maybe there are times when you feel an urge to do something creative, to play, to dance. But some nagging inner voice is saying, "You should finish this or that work first. There is no time to play." Or perhaps you feel anger welling up within yourself, and a voice within says, "You shouldn't feel this way; it's wrong. You're just being selfish." Or maybe you do not like the way your life is going, and you would like to trust God and open your hands to him. Then that nagging inner voice says, "You should know what you need for your own happiness. You have asked God to give it to you and he has not. You should forget about him. He does not care about you."

There is a name for the disease that these nagging inner voices inflict on our child. It is called "Should Fever." It describes all the things we or other people think we *should* be in contrast to what we can and want to be. It saps the strength of our inner child, and when left unchecked it can bring on a mortal illness.

Now let us consider the figure of Jairus, the little girl's father. Can you identify a Jairus within yourself? An adult part of yourself who cares deeply and who tries to combat the Should Fever in every way he can? An inner self who recognizes the seriousness of the illness and is willing to take risks to obtain fullness of life for your child? One who rushes to seek the help of Jesus? Perhaps you can recognize Jairus in your resistance to the Shoulds. Maybe Jairus is that something within you that refuses to accept the final victory of the disease. Perhaps he is that part of you which recognizes that you have done all that you can do, and now it is up to the Lord to restore life and to return your child to full participation in the unfolding of your true self.

Of course, it is vital to be aware of the presence and concern of Jesus throughout the scene. He is available and ready to respond to the call to come to the aid of our child. Jesus is eager and willing to restore to us the cherished child who is so vital to our entering into the fullness of life that is the kingdom of God. It is important to remember that, beyond the restoration of life, Jesus is concerned that our inner child receive our continual nurturing. His final statement at the closing of the scene is a simple command, "Give her something to eat."

Step 4—Meditation

Now that we have re-created the event in our imagination and then attemped to identify Jairus and his child as parts of our inner selves, let us enter into dialogue with them in meditation. This time, you might try writing out the dialogue. Writing can be a very helpful technique in getting into a meditation and helping it move forward. If writing is not effective for you, you might simply imagine the dialogue. However, even if writing is not helpful for you this time, it may be at another time, so you may wish to try it again. The important thing about any technique in meditation is that it is simply a means to an end. If it works, use it; if it does not work, try something else that is effective for you.

Meditative writing is different from other kinds of writing. We begin as suggested in Chapter 1 to prepare for meditation, using whichever techniques are helpful to become quiet and centered. At this level of increased awareness the writing, which may seem to be an active outer activity, can become simply an instrument of expression for our inner selves. It can be a key to unlocking the door between outer and inner reality.

Now read the passage once again. Imagine the scene and let it unfold. Choose one of the figures of the story and begin a conversation with him or her. Write out the dialogue. Often it is helpful to begin writing just anything, even if you feel uninspired. A good way to get started is to ask a question of the character you have chosen, and begin writing out his/her response. Remember that Jairus and his child are parts of your inner self.

Here are some questions you might want to try to help you get started:

To Jairus:

How do you feel now, as you ask Jesus to come to help your little girl?

How do you feel about Jesus' ability to help her?

What part of your child do you think is dying? (Perhaps growing ability, playfulness, sensitivity to feelings, trust)

What are the Shoulds that are making her ill?

What kind of nourishment do you think she needs to stay well and grow?

To the child:

What is your name: (Playfulness? Joy? Trust?)

What are you like?

What caused your sickness/death?

What kind of nourishment do you need to keep you well and growing?

To Jesus:

How do you feel toward Jairus?

How do you feel toward the child?

What do you think the child is like?

What caused her illness?

What kind of nourishment does she need now?

If you reach a point where the flow of dialogue bogs down, you might try closing your eyes and becoming still again, as you did at the beginning of your meditation. Visualize the scene at the point where your dialogue stopped. Get in touch with the feelings of the characters. Experience them as parts of yourself. Either let the action go forward in this way or begin writing again. It is often quite worthwhile to let the scene progress beyond the end of the actual scripture passage.

It might be productive to return to this passage from time

to time for reflection and meditation. Children are prone to a variety of illnesses, and our inner child is no exception. At one time, our child may be stricken with the Growth-Stunting kind of Should Fever, another time with the Playfulness-Squelching or Emotion-Suppressing variety, and yet another time with the Suspicion strain of the Should Fever virus, to which our Trusting Child is especially susceptible. So our inner child needs our continuing attention and nurturing, as well as repeated healing and revival. The passage provides imagery which can be a powerful aid in keeping our inner child alive and vibrant and growing.

The keeping of a journal can be especially effective in our continuing effort to nurture our inner child. In a journal, we record our innermost thoughts and feelings, our dreams and meditation imagery, our significant life experiences. We can then look back from time to time, and often we are able to gain a deeper insight into the meaning of our experiences. For example, we may have viewed a particular experience as a shameful personal failure at the time it occurred. Or we may have had an especially painful experience in which we could find no meaning. Looking back, we may realize that we learned much from the experience and that it presented us with an opportunity for new growth. It can be easier to accept and cherish our failures and pain when we see them in retrospect, as stages in our growth toward fullness of life.

A journal can also function as an early-detection aid in diagnosing an attack of Should Fever. Through the perspective of a period of time recorded in our journal, we can sometimes perceive patterns of behavior or attitudes which are symptoms of a form of Should Fever. We can then take steps to halt the progress of the disease before our inner child becomes seriously ill.

Together with the imagery of the story of Jairus and his child, a journal can be an important aid in enabling us to bring to full fruition our own unique inner resources.

4

A FATHER & TWO SONS

Let us look at the familiar parable of the Prodigal Son, Luke 15:11–32 (New American Bible):

Jesus said to them: "A man had two sons. The younger of them said to his father, 'Father, give me the share of the estate that is coming to me.' So the father divided up the property. Some days later this younger son collected all his belongings and went off to a distant land, where he squandered his money on dissolute living. After he had spent everything, a great famine broke out in that country and he was in dire need. So he attached himself to one of the propertied class of the place, who sent him to his farm to take care of the pigs. He longed to fill his belly with the husks that were fodder for the pigs, but no one made a move to give him anything. Coming to his senses at last, he said: 'How many hired hands at my father's place have more than enough to eat, while here I am starving! I will break away and return to my father, and say to him, Father, I have sinned against God and against you; I no longer deserve to be called your son. Treat me like one of your hired hands.' With that he set off for his father's house. While he was still a long way off, his father caught sight of him and was deeply moved. He ran out to meet him, threw his arms around his neck, and kissed him. The son said to him, 'Father, I have sinned against God and against you; I no longer deserve to be called your son.' The father said to his servants: 'Quick! bring out the finest robe and put it on him; put a ring on his finger and shoes on his feet. Take the fatted calf and kill it. Let us eat and celebrate, because this son of mine was dead and has come back to life. He was lost and is found.' Then the celebration began.

"Meanwhile the elder son was out on the land. As he neared the house on his way home, he heard the sound of music and dancing. He called one of the servants and asked him the reason for the dancing and the music. The servant answered, 'Your brother is home, and your father has killed the fatted calf because he has him back in good health.' The son grew angry at this and would not go in; but his father came out and began to plead with him.

"He said to his father in reply: 'For years now I have slaved for you. I never disobeyed one of your orders, yet you never gave me so much as a kid goat to celebrate with my friends. Then, when this son of yours returns after having gone through your property with loose women, you kill the fatted calf for him.'

" 'My son,' replied the father, 'you are with me always, and everything I have is yours. But we had to celebrate and rejoice! This brother of yours was dead, and has come back to life. He was lost, and is found.' "

We will consider the passage in four steps, as before.

Step 1—Scriptural Background

There are several points in the parable that would be understood by Jesus' Jewish audience in ways that could be signficant in a search for the inner meaning of the passage:

a. The younger son's job of caring for the pigs would be

considered just about the most degrading work a Jew could do, the lowest point to which he could sink—the bottom of the pit.

b. In the culture of the time, it would have been considered undignified and humiliating for the father of a household to go out to greet someone the way this father ran out to greet his younger son.

c. The clothing which the father provides for his son is significant. The finest robe is usually reserved for distinguished guests and special occasions. The ring and shoes are signs of sonship; only the servants went barefoot.

d. The angry reference of the elder son to "this son of yours" in verse 30 is noteworthy. It is a bitter denial of any relationship with his younger brother. In verse 32, the father gently rebukes his elder son for his unbrotherly attitude by referring to "this brother of yours."

Step 2—Re-creating the Event

Imagine the changing feelings of each character as the story unfolds. How do you think the younger son feels as he asks his father for his share of the estate? Apprehensive? Nervous? Confident? Daring? How do you think he feels as he sets out on his journey? Courageous? Excited? Worried? Torn? Free? How about his feelings as he spends his money living recklessly? Happy? Ecstatic? Playful? Carefree? What about his feelings when he ends up with the pigs? Disillusioned? Lonely? Stupid? Worthless? Guilty? Confused? Helpless? Angry? Hopeless? Afraid? How might he feel as he decides to return to his father? Hopeful? Ashamed? Apprehensive? Fearful? Foolish? How do you think he feels as his father runs to him, embraces and forgives him, and calls for the banquet? Incredulous? Bewildered? Relieved? Overjoyed? Secure? Warm? Loved?

Now let us consider the feelings of the elder son. What emotions do you think he experiences as he learns of his brother's return and of the celebration? Angry? Jealous? Betrayed? Bitter? Hurt?

What emotions might the father have been experiencing

as his younger son left home? Worried? Sad? Understanding? Torn? Resigned? How does he feel as he sees his son returning in the distance and as he embraces him? Joyous? Elated? Loving? Sympathetic? Relieved? How might the father feel as he urges his elder son to join the celebration? Understanding? Compassionate? Loving? Anxious?

Step 3—Inner Meaning

This parable is considered to be a key statement of Jesus' view of God as Father. It is also a description of the basic human journey toward wholeness. As such, it deserves some very special attention.

In order to find the inner meaning of the parable for ourselves, we need to consider several aspects of the story. First, we need to recognize our own inner prodigal son and elder brother. Second, we need to identify the similarities between our own inner journeys and the journeys of the two sons. Third, we need to look at God our Father as he is represented by the father of the parable, and then seek to understand our own relationship with God in the light of the "parable-portrait" of him.

Let us look at the two sons and attempt to identify our own inner prodigal son and his elder brother. Recalling the emotions you think the prodigal experiences as the parable progresses, you can probably recognize similar feelings in your own experience. Like this son, we feel a sense of failure, shame or worthlessness at times, and also find it hard to imagine that God our Father could be so totally forgiving and loving. We also have within us an elder son who cannot understand or accept the father's generosity. Perhaps both inner sons are most easily recognized in the conflict between them—the prodigal side of us seeking to be reconciled and whole, yet hardly daring to hope that we are worthy, the older brother side of us certain that we are not worthy and even wanting to deny any relationship between these parts of ourself.

Both our inner prodigal and his older brother are valuable

parts of ourselves. Our prodigal is that which is open to risk and yet able to turn around out of failure and shame toward God our Father. Our older brother points out ways in which we have thoughtlessly caused pain or hurt, and sees the value of the traditional and stable elements of life. God calls us to cherish each of these inner sons as he does, and urges us to reconcile the two of them.

Now let us consider the journeys of the two sons. A journey involves movement from one place to another, leaving something behind and coming to a new place. It means leaving a known environment and entering into an unknown situation, and therefore involves some risk. An inner journey is similar. It is a movement, a change, a growth. Something is left behind, such as an attitude or a habit. There is a letting go, a kind of death. There is often pain or confusion, a darkness, a difficulty in letting go and an anxiety about the unknown ahead. There is an arrival at a new place, and there is new life and light.

These elements are present in the journey of the prodigal son. His physical journey is an image of the inner human journey or time of growth. He makes a decision to leave behind the security of his home, risking disapproval and possibly even disownment by his father, and heads into an unknown situation. Things do not work out as he had planned—a familiar human experience! He experiences pain and loneliness, darkness, and dire need. Just as we are often able to see things differently when we are in great need, so also the prodigal, out of his need, is able to see in a new way the value of his father's home. He is even willing to accept the status of servant just for the security and nourishment of home. But then he finds a surprise—which is another common element of our inner journey. We find something we could not even imagine at the beginning. The prodigal hardly dares hope to be accepted even as a servant, and then finds his father not only welcoming him with open arms and restoring him to full sonship, but celebrating with a banquet! He sees something he could not see before—the extravagance of his father's love. He comes out of darkness to light, out of death to a new life, and that is the way our inner journeys are.

The journey of the elder son is less obvious. He moves physically and routinely from the fields to the house, to be nourished regularly at his father's table. There is no indication of any inner journey or growth occurring. But then on the day of his brother's return, an invitation is extended by his father to begin an inner journey. His father pleads with him to come into the house, be reconciled with his brother, and celebrate with them. The journey from the outside to the inside of the house could be an arduous and risky one for the elder brother. He would have to work through his anger and jealousy, leave behind his limited sense of values, work through his confusion to discern what is truly valuable in his traditional thinking, risk letting go of some of his pre-conceived ideas, and face the challenge of a changed but revitalized relationship with his father and his brother. That is the kind of journey to which our Father invites our inner elder brother.

There is something else about the journeys of the two sons which is similar to our inner journeys. The younger son begins his journey out of an inner urging, while his elder brother is called to a journey as a result of an outer event—the return of his brother and the resultant celebration. This seems to be true of the growth or journey times of our lives. It does not seem to matter whether our urging to move and to grow comes from within ourselves or results from an outer circumstance. What matters is how we respond—whether or not we choose to grow and learn and move on to a new place, and whether or not we arrive at a point of inner peace and reconciliation.

Now let us focus our attention on the figure of the father in the story to see the similarities with God our Father. The father of the parable is full of surprises from start to finish. He seems to do just what he would be least expected to do. He gives his younger son the freedom to take his inheritance and leave home. He eagerly and hopefully watches for his return.

He ignores the etiquette of the time and manifests his great joy by running out to embrace his son as he returns. He does not scold him, or turn him away as might be expected. The father does not even let his son finish his prepared speech; he will not listen to his talk about no longer deserving to be called a son. He only wants his son to turn around and come back. Then he holds a lavish celebration, a banquet in his honor. That is far beyond expectations also, considering the insult and hurt his younger son has caused.

The father also responds to his elder son's expressions of anger and jealousy in an unexpected way. He encourages him to love and forgive his brother and pleads with him to join in the celebration.

It is as if the father is seeing his two sons when they were learning to walk—knowing they must stumble in the process—encouraging them and loving them throughout the learning—waiting with open arms to embrace them. He knows his younger son will stumble but he also knows he must find his own way—and he loves him with a constant love throughout the process, waiting with open arms for his return.

The father likewise stands before his elder son, watching him stumble through his anger and jealousy—encouraging him to take a first step and begin to walk in love and forgiveness.

And so the "parable-portrait" of God our Father emerges, showing him to be a God who loves us constantly and abundantly, who cherishes us just as much when we stumble in failure as when we walk tall in success, and who loves to surprise us. This extravagant, constant love of God for us is one of the hardest things for us to believe in sometimes—and one of the greatest challenges to our faith. Our inability to believe in the depth of God's love for us can be a formidable barrier in growing to our fullest potential. If we fear God's punishment or are unconvinced of his total love and care for us, we are inhibited from rising up and trying again. We recoil rather than risk another step. We become imprisoned in our own fear and insecurity. We are blinded from seeing God's open arms and loving face.

The destination in the journeys of both of our inner sons is the same: the home of God our Father. He pleads with us and encourages us to come in to the banquet and become reconciled and whole within ourselves, enabled by the strength and nourishment of his great love for us.

As we pass through the inner growing stages of our life, we need to return again and again to our Father, drawn ever onward by our belief that he is always waiting with open arms to embrace us as his beloved daughters and sons.

Step 4—Meditation

Recalling the changing emotions of the main figures of the parable, slowly read the passage again. Try to be keenly aware of all the ways the father expresses the lavishness of his love for both of his sons.

Now take a few minutes to relax and become quiet, using whatever techniques you find helpful. Then let the story unfold in your imagination. Let the two sons be parts of yourself, and see the father as God. Let the story progress at its own pace, lingering where it will. Write out some dialogue if that is helpful. Let the story continue in your imagination beyond the end of the gospel passage itself. Throughout your meditation, try to feel deeply the warmth and intensity of God's love for you, especially for both the younger and older sons within you. If you have trouble accepting the unconditional, total love of God for you, you might want to talk it over with your Father. Try to free yourself to accept his embrace and allow him to place his finest robe around your shoulders, a ring on your finger and shoes on your feet. Try to go with him into the banquet and receive his nourishment. Allow God to bring your own inner prodigal and elder brother together in love, to share in the celebration of the returning of both sons to the Father and to each other. You were dead and have come back to life. You were lost and are found. Celebrate! Rejoice!

Another Meditation

Following is a guided meditation—a reflection on the Our Father. Prepare for it by becoming relaxed and quiet, as before. Then read through it slowly, letting images arise and flow as they will. Stop and linger at any part that is especially meaningful to you.

OUR FATHER, WHO ART IN HEAVEN . . .

>   . . . Jesus taught us to call you ABBA.
>   . . . I believe that you love and care for me as a good father for a little child.
>   . . . I believe that your love for me is lavish and never-faltering, that you love me no matter what mistakes I make. Father, ABBA, help my unbelief.
>   . . . Help me to believe that you are really like the father of the prodigal son—that you are extravagant in your love for me—that you give me the freedom to stumble and to learn from my stumbling.
>   . . . Help me to believe that you are waiting with open arms to welcome me back when I am lost in my own shame or fear or sense of worthlessness.
>   . . . I open my arms to you as you embrace me—as you clothe me as your beloved son/daughter—as you dance and rejoice with me in the new life and the warmth to which I have returned.

HALLOWED BE THY NAME . . .

>   . . . Thank you for being there with me, Father, all along the way.
>   . . . I sing . . . and dance . . . to the glory of your name.

THY KINGDOM COME . . .

>   . . . May your reign of love enter fully into my life and the life of all people.

... May the vision of wholeness that is your kingdom unite all of us in love.

THY WILL BE DONE ON EARTH AS IT IS IN HEAVEN ...
... Father, ABBA, do I dare to believe that there are no limits to the possibilities of your kingdom on earth?
... Dare I believe that even now I can begin to enter into that fullness of life that we call heaven?
... Help me remove from myself, one by one, the limits I have placed on the fullness of your kingdom on earth.

GIVE US THIS DAY OUR DAILY BREAD ...
... I need your nourishment, Father, for my journey from darkness to light, from death to life.
... Take my hand, Father ... be my strength ... show me the way.
... You are always near, I know ... ready to give me whatever I need for each part of my journey.
... Father, I need strength ... strength to keep my hands open to receive the daily gifts you offer to me ... for your gifts are not always what I expect ... or what I think I need.
... Father, ABBA, help me to trust you completely, to believe that the gifts you give are always beyond my imagining ... and always a surprise.

AND FORGIVE US OUR TRESPASSES ...
... I wander away from the path of light so often, Father.
... You are so accepting ... so patient ... as you see me search and stumble.
... Help me to forgive myself so that I may feel deeply your love for me, no matter where I am on my journey.

AS WE FORGIVE THOSE WHO TRESPASS AGAINST US ...
... Father, help me to look upon others with the same

warmth and concern as you do . . .
as they also walk . . .
and sometimes falter . . .
along the path of their life . . .
and no matter where they are
on their journey.

AND LEAD US NOT INTO TEMPTATION, BUT DELIVER
US FROM EVIL . . .
. . . Take my hand again, Father, ABBA.
. . . Guide me along my way.
. . . Protect me from myself when I am tempted to doubt
your love.
. . . Light my way. Show me the next step on my journey.
. . . Shine the light and warmth of your love on my own inner self, so that where I am divided I may be reconciled, where I am lost I may be found, and where I am
dead I may return to life.

FOR THE KINGDOM,
AND THE POWER,
AND THE GLORY ARE YOURS,
NOW AND FOREVER.
AMEN.   ALLELUIA!

5

THE BLIND, THE LAME
& THE SICK

As mentioned in the first chapter, there are many myths that contain the kind of universal imagery which can lead us into contact with our inner selves. One such myth is the old, familiar story of *Beauty and the Beast.* It can be a helpful step in approaching the inner meaning of the group of gospel passages we will explore in this chapter.

In the story of *Beauty and the Beast,* Beauty has agreed to live with Beast in exchange for Beast sparing the life of her father. Beauty is afraid of Beast and repelled by his ugliness. Beast is ferocious and easily angered by her rejection. He asks her to marry him, an idea which totally repels her. As the story progresses, a gradual change occurs in their relationship. Beauty begins to detect a goodness and gentleness underneath Beast's exterior ugliness and wildness. As she begins to respond to him with less fear and to show that she sees some value in him, Beast becomes less ferocious and more patient. When Beast asks her to marry him, she still cannot accept, but is gentler and more regretful in her refusal.

Later, Beauty leaves Beast for a visit to her home. When she returns to Beast, she is shocked to find him dying. She realizes that she truly loves him and tells him she will marry him if he recovers. He is then transformed into a handsome prince. His exterior appearance now expresses the inner goodness and value that Beauty had perceived hidden beneath his outer ugliness.

We all have our inner beasts—those parts of ourselves which we hate and fear, whose existence we deny or hide. They look ugly to us. They frighten and repel us. When we look honestly at our inner beasts, accept them as parts of ourselves and finally love them, they become transformed into true royalty. This in turn leads to greater understanding and compassion for others. When the beasts in others are expressed outwardly, we are better able to see their hidden goodness, to love them and thus enable them to transform their beastly trait into its royal counterpart.

For example, suppose I sometimes feel jealous, but I am not aware of it. I cannot consciously admit it. Then I begin to perceive it. I finally see that I am capable of feeling jealous. Perhaps with great effort, I accept this as part of myself. In so doing, I become free to respond differently to the feeling. I also can see and cherish the counterpart of my jealousy—its other side—perhaps my ability to love intensely. I can then nurture this aspect of myself and respond more consciously to feelings of jealousy that do arise. Likewise, when I perceive jealousy in others, I am able to see the other side of it—the ability to care deeply. I can understand and respond with compassion, thus providing a climate wherein others are more likely to be able to be aware of and accept their jealous side and to nurture its counterpart in themselves.

There are many stories in the gospels that involve people to whom others respond with fear or revulsion. These are the lepers, the crippled, the blind—all those who experience physical disorders, who lack physical well-being and wholeness. Jesus responds to them with compassion. He touches and heals them.

The particular type of sickness or deformity involved in each healing story can help us to more clearly define the specific kind of beastliness we need to attend to at a particular time—for we all have our own inner deformed and rejected parts, our inner paralytic or leper or blind or deaf self. When we reject or ignore these dark parts of ourself, they turn on us, repel and frighten us, possess us or paralyze us. When we are able to consciously attend to them, accept and love them, we turn toward the Lord and are enabled to receive his healing touch. Then they are transformed into the royally beautiful and creative parts of ourselves that they were meant to be. They are brought out of shadow and darkness into light, out of death into life.

We will approach the selected group of six healing stories in a slightly different way from the previous passages. We have already considered the inner meaning of the stories in a general way. Now we will take each passage individually and consider the first three steps together: the scriptural background, re-creation of the event, and specific inner meaning. Then we will consider general suggestions for meditation which will apply to the stories as a group.

Let us first consider the story of the healing of a paralytic, Matthew 9:1–8 (New American Bible):

Then he reentered the boat, made the crossing, and came back to his own town. There the people at once brought to him a paralyzed man lying on a mat. When Jesus saw their faith he said to the paralytic, "Have courage, son, your sins are forgiven." At that some of the scribes said to themselves, "The man blasphemes." Jesus was aware of what they were thinking and said: "Why do you harbor evil thoughts? Which is less trouble to say, 'Your sins are forgiven' or 'Stand up and walk'? To help you realize that the Son of Man has authority on earth to forgive sins"—he then said to the paralyzed man—"Stand up! Roll up your mat, and go home." The man stood up and went toward his home. At the sight, a feeling of awe came over the crowd, and they praised God for giving such authority to men.

The Jews viewed physical sickness to be a result of sin. Thus, if a person's sins were forgiven, he or she could be healed. This view is not as archaic as it may seem. As mentioned in Chapter 3, when we deny or suppress our emotions they are likely to be expressed as physical illness. We fail to forgive ourselves for our "bad" feelings and we become ill! We become paralyzed by fear, guilt or anger. We need to forgive and accept ourselves in order to be able to be healed. Only then will we be able to arise and walk and be free to move on to the next stage of our growth.

How might the paralytic be feeling? Helpless? Confused? Out of control? And what about the scribes? Threatened? Disbelieving? Skeptical?

We need to identify the paralytic within ourselves, perhaps by identifying with his feelings. We also need to identify our inner scribes—that which does not believe we can be healed, or feels threatened by the power of the Lord. We need to let the voice of our inner scribes help us identify the area of our own unbelief, so that we can then face and accept our inner paralytic and enable ourselves to become opened to the healing power of the Lord.

Now let us turn to the account of the healing of a possessed mute, Matthew 9:32–33 (New American Bible):

As they were leaving, suddenly some people brought him a mute who was possessed by a demon. Once the demon was expelled the mute began to speak, to the great surprise of the crowds. "Nothing like this has ever been seen in Israel!" they exclaimed. But the Pharisees were saying, "He casts out demons through the prince of demons."

Muteness, i.e., dumbness or inability to speak, implies deafness also, in the scriptural usage. Let us explore how the deaf mute might feel. Isolated? Lonely? Helpless? Misunderstood? We need to get in touch with our own inner deaf mute, perhaps through such questions as: "How am I deaf and dumb—unable to hear myself and others—unable to speak of who I really am, my true feelings? How do I feel thus possessed? Isolated in my lack of communication of my true self?" Let us not overlook our inner Pharisee, skeptically disbelieving that we can be healed and freed from our isolation. We need to hear our inner Pharisee's accusations and deal with the resulting conflict. As in the story of the adulteress in Chapter 2, we need to hear our Pharisee but also know when to stop listening and turn to Jesus. We need to overcome our own disbelief and accept the power of Jesus to touch and heal us.

Now let us consider a story of the healing of a leper, Mark 1:40–42 (New American Bible):

> A leper approached him with a request, kneeling down as he addressed him: "If you will to do so, you can cure me." Moved with pity, Jesus stretched out his hand, touched him, and said: "I do will it. Be cured." The leprosy left him then and there, and he was cured.

A leper in biblical times was considered "unclean." He or she was required to be separated from the community, refrain from touching others, and warn of his or her approach by ringing a bell and calling out, "Unclean." The leper was looked upon with revulsion and dread. Jesus' touching of the leper is all the more remarkable in light of this attitude.

What emotions might the leper be experiencing? Isolation? Depression? Worthlessness? Rejection? Hopelessness? Our own experience of similar feelings can help us identify our own inner leper. Perhaps we could ask ourselves if there is a part of ourselves which we look upon with revulsion and fear, a part which we reject and view as untouchable. Perhaps we can begin to see our inner leper as Jesus does, with compassion and understanding. We can try to reach out and touch our leper, cherish and embrace this rejected and ailing part of ourselves—and thus open ourselves to the healing touch of Jesus.

Let us turn now to the account of Jesus' healing of a man with a withered hand, Mark 3:1–5 (New American Bible):

> He returned to the synagogue where there was a man whose hand was shriveled up. They kept an eye on Jesus to see whether he would heal him on the sabbath, hoping to be able to bring an accusation against him. He addressed the man with the shriveled hand: "Stand up here in front!" Then he said to them: "Is it permitted to do a good deed on the sabbath—or an evil one? To preserve life—or to destroy it?" At this they remained silent. He looked around at them with anger, for he was deeply grieved that they had closed their minds against him. Then he said to the man, "Stretch out your hand." The man did so and his hand was perfectly restored.

We might ask ourselves in what ways we feel crippled, helpless, unable to function—and thus discover our own inner deformity. Also, let us not overlook our inner Pharisee, who as usual is creating a conflict and possibly detouring us from Jesus' healing and our coming to greater wholeness.

Consider also the story of the woman with a hemorrhage, Mark 5:25–34 (New American Bible):

> There was a woman in the area who had been afflicted with a hemorrhage for a dozen years. She had received treatment at the hands of doctors of every sort and exhausted her savings in the process, yet she got no relief; on the contrary, she only grew worse. She had heard about Jesus and came up behind him in the crowd and put her hand to his cloak. "If I just touch

his clothing," she thought, "I shall get well." Immediately her flow of blood dried up and the feeling that she was cured of her affliction ran through her whole body. Jesus was conscious at once that healing power had gone out from him. Wheeling about in the crowd, he began to ask, "Who touched my clothing?" His disciples said to him, "You can see how this crowd hems you in, yet you ask, 'Who touched me?'" Despite this, he kept looking around to see the woman who had done it. Fearful and beginning to tremble now as she realized what had happened, the woman came and fell in front of him and told him the whole truth. He said to her, "Daughter, it is your faith that has cured you. Go in peace and be free of this illness."

Blood has such a very deep significance. It is the sign of life, that which brings nourishment to our entire body. The woman of the story must have felt weak, discouraged, drained. Let us search for any part of ourselves that feels drained of the flow of life. Let us urge that part of ourself to reach toward Jesus in our search for wholeness and fullness of life.

The last healing story we will explore is the account of Jesus' meeting with the blind Bartimaeus, Mark 10:46–52 (New American Bible):

They came to Jericho next, and as he was leaving that place with his disciples and a sizable crowd, there was a blind beggar Bartimaeus ("son of Timaeus") sitting by the roadside. On hearing that it was Jesus of Nazareth, he began to call out, "Jesus, Son of David, have pity on me!" Many people were scolding him to make him keep quiet, but he shouted all the louder, "Son of David, have pity on me!" Then Jesus stopped and said, "Call him over." So they called the blind man over, telling him as they did so, "You have nothing to fear from him! Get up! He is calling you!" He threw aside his cloak, jumped up and came to Jesus. Jesus asked

him, "What do you want me to do for you?" "Rabbo-
ni," the blind man said, "I want to see." Jesus said in
reply, "Be on your way. Your faith has healed you."
Immediately he received his sight and started to follow him up the road.

Let us look inward and attempt to discern our own blind-
nesses, asking what it is that we are unable or unwilling to see.
We may feel a frustration at being unable to understand, or a
fear that we may not be able to handle what we might see.
Perhaps there is a part of us, like the crowd, that scolds and
tries to quiet our blind self as it cries out for sight. Perhaps
there is a part of ourself that can calm our fears as did some of
the crowd. We may need to urge our blind self to be persistent
like Bartimaeus. It may feel risky to say honestly, "I want to
see." We may instinctively realize that in asking for sight we
become vulnerable—open to the possibility of being called to
further growth. It is significant that immediately after the restoring of his sight to Bartimaeus, Jesus enters Jerusalem and
the climax of his ministry—his passion, death and resurrection—and that Bartimaeus follows him. It is not easy to respond to our inner call to clearer vision, for it is almost certain
to be followed by a call to deeper participation in the mystery
of death and resurrection. Our reflection on this passage can
help us to work through our inner conflicts in our journey
toward new life and growth.

Meditation

Reflecting on these six healing stories, choose the one that
seems most meaningful to you right now. Rather than doing
too much thinking about it, let your inner urgings do the
choosing if possible. Become quiet and relaxed. If one of the
stories stands out from the others, focus on it. If not, briefly re-
view all the stories and choose the one that seems to attract
you the most, or the one that expresses that inner part of you
that is most in need of healing right now. It is important to

choose only one of the stories for now. You can return to the others at a later time.

After you have chosen one of the stories, identify the feelings of the main characters in the story. Name the emotions and write them down. Then, if possible, identify a specific outer experience that expresses the presence of your inner paralytic, leper, crippled or otherwise disabled self.

Become quiet and relaxed again. Close your eyes and let the story unfold in your imagination, with the characters being your own inner selves. You might want to have a dialogue with Jesus or with the inner selves you have chosen. Stop a moment when you come before Jesus for healing. Try to look at your own crippled or injured or ill part in the way Jesus looks at you. Feel the same compassion and love for yourself that he does. Reach out to yourself with him and touch the needy and painful parts of yourself with his healing hand. Allow yourself to be open to his touch. Allow yourself to be transformed into his image and likeness.

It would be worthwhile to return to this meditation from time to time, using a different story each time. We are constantly in need of inner healing. It is part of our human growth process, and urges us on to further growth and fuller life. The part of our inner self that needs healing varies with our life experiences. One or another of the healing stories can usually help us focus on the neediest parts of ourselves and help to accelerate our growth.

Another Meditation

This is a guided meditation. The settings are the hill of Calvary, the tomb, and the place in which the disciples had locked themselves after the death of Jesus (John 20:19–21). Imagine you are one of the disciples. Remember to stop and linger at any point that is particularly meaningful to you.

Gently close your eyes. Become comfortable, quiet, relaxed. Let the stillness surround you. Breathe gently, slowly. Breathe out the tensions and turbulence of the day. Breathe in

the deep stillness of God's presence. When you are ready, open
your eyes and slowly read the following. You may want to close
your eyes again and reflect on a certain point, going on only
when you have exhausted it.

Imagine a hill near the city of Jerusalem . . .
    the hill of Calvary . . .
    the place of the crucifixion.
    We are there together . . .
        at the foot of the cross.
    We feel so helpless.
        We are losing him.
        Jesus is dying . . .
            and there is nothing we can do.
        We can only stand by . . .
            and hear him breathe his last breath . . .
            and know that we have lost him . . .
            know that he is gone.

Gently, we take his lifeless body from the cross.
    We carry him to the tomb,
        and lay him on the stone slab.
    We look at him . . .
        so white, so cold, so lifeless.
    And then the memories come flooding over us.
        How warm he was, just a few days ago,
            a few hours ago.
        He was so full of life . . .
            and we were just beginning to feel some
            of that life flowing through ourselves.
        He knew us so well . . .
            so much better than we knew ourselves.
        And he loved us, as no one else ever had.
        We were just beginning

to really believe in ourselves . . .
and to love ourselves.
And we were just beginning to be able
to love the people he loved.
He seemed to love such strange people.
We were not accustomed to loving
the kind of people he loved.
He touched them . . .
and he healed them . . .
with his love.

All kinds of people were beginning to be able to live and
to love more than they ever thought they could.
We were just beginning to realize that all those other
people . . .
the ones we could not love very easily . . .
were like parts of ourselves . . .
our own inner adulteress . . . blind person . . .
leper . . . paralytic.
And we began to believe that we could love even
those shadowy, dark parts of ourselves.
We were all being healed.
We were being restored to life.
And now this.
Our lives are suddenly turned upside down.
And we feel so alone.

We leave the tomb.
We cling to each other for comfort, for strength.
We go to a place where we can be alone.
We huddle together in a room . . .
with the doors locked.

Then gradually our grief and loneliness are pushed aside
by a new feeling.

We are afraid.
     He is gone too soon.
          Are we going to be able to keep on living and
               loving without him?
          He was so strong, so confident.
               He was always there for us when we were
                    confused . . . and hurt . . .
                    or angry . . . or afraid.
                    And what now?

And then . . . we see him!
     Here . . . in our midst!
          We did not see him come in.
          It is almost as if he had been here all along . . .
               and only just now were we able to see him.

Now, for a moment, imagine how Jesus looks.
     Let the fullness of his life fill you with warmth.
     Let the brightness of his light reach to the
          darkest corners of your inmost depths . . .
               dispelling the shadows . . .
                    filling you with light . . .
               bringing to your vision
                    all the goodness and beauty within you . . .
                    all the strength and wisdom
                    and love hidden there.
     Look and see the image of God within yourself.
                    Amen.   Alleluia!

6

BREAD & WINE

Let us look at the account of the two disciples on the road to
Emmaus. The story takes place after the resurrection and after
the women had been to the tomb, Luke 24:13–35 (New American Bible):

> Two of them that same day were making their way to
> a village named Emmaus seven miles distant from Je-
> rusalem, discussing as they went all that had hap-
> pened. In the course of their lively exchange, Jesus
> approached and began to walk along with them. How-
> ever, they were restrained from recognizing him. He
> said to them, "What are you discussing as you go your
> way?" They halted, in distress, and one of them, Cleo-
> pas by name, asked him, "Are you the only resident of
> Jerusalem who does not know the things that went on
> there these past few days?" He said to them, "What
> things?" They said, "All those that had to do with Je-
> sus of Nazareth, a prophet powerful in word and deed
> in the eyes of God and all the people; how our chief
> priests and leaders delivered him up to be con-
> demned to death, and crucified him. We were hoping
> that he was the one who would set Israel free. Besides

all this, today, the third day since these things happened, some women of our group have just brought us some astonishing news. They were at the tomb before dawn and failed to find his body, but returned with the tale that they had seen a vision of angels who declared he was alive. Some of our number went to the tomb and found it to be just as the women said; but him they did not see."

Then he said to them, "What little sense you have! How slow you are to believe all that the prophets have announced! Did not the Messiah have to undergo all this so as to enter into his glory?" Beginning, then, with Moses and all the prophets, he interpreted for them every passage of Scripture which referred to him. By now they were near the village to which they were going, and he acted as if he were going farther. But they pressed him: "Stay with us. It is nearly evening—the day is practically over." So he went in to stay with them.

When he had seated himself with them to eat, he took bread, pronounced the blessing, then broke the bread and began to distribute it to them. With that their eyes were opened and they recognized him; whereupon he vanished from their sight. They said to one another, "Were not our hearts burning inside us as he talked to us on the road and explained the Scriptures to us?" They got up immediately and returned to Jerusalem, where they found the Eleven and the rest of the company assembled. They were greeted with "The Lord has been raised! It is true! He has appeared to Simon." Then they recounted what had happened on the road and how they had come to know him in the breaking of bread.

This story is a reflection of the eucharistic celebration. At the Eucharist we celebrate the presence of the risen Lord among us. We express our own participation in the mystery of his death and resurrection. The structure of the story reflects the basic structure of the Eucharist. First, there is a focus on the presence of the Lord in the scriptural word. As the two disciples were drawn to Jesus through the scriptures, their "hearts burning inside" them, so we too are drawn ever nearer the Lord as he is revealed to us in the liturgy of the word.

Second, the two disciples recognized the risen Christ in "the breaking of bread." This reflects our own recognition of the presence of Christ in the liturgy of the Eucharist—expressed in the signs of bread and wine. The early Christians referred to the eucharistic celebration—including both the sharing of the scriptural word and the breaking of the bread and the sharing of the wine—as simply "the breaking of the bread."

We have been inclined to limit our experience of the presence of the Lord in the eucharistic bread and wine to an intellectual understanding. We can expand our experience by exploring the meaning of bread and wine from a fuller human perspective.

The incarnation means that in experiencing Jesus in his humanity we experience divinity. The more fully we experience our own humanity, the more deeply we can relate to Jesus' humanity—and the more fully we can find God within that human experience.

In searching for the fuller meanings of bread and wine, then, we will first probe our own human experience of these simple gifts. We will explore bread and wine as signs of who we are and who we can be within ourselves and to each other. Then we will look at them as signs of who Jesus is and thus be able to perceive them more fully as expressions of his risen presence among us.

Let us begin with Jesus' own stated meaning of the bread and wine. He said of the bread, "This is my body"—and broke and shared the bread. The Jews of Jesus' time made no distinction between body and soul; that idea was Greek in origin and came later. A person's body was understood as the whole person. In saying, "Take and eat; this is my body," Jesus was offering himself to become one with us as bread becomes one with the person who consumes it.

Jesus said of the cup of wine, "This is my blood"—and shared the cup with his apostles. Blood symbolized life to the Jews. So Jesus offered himself—his whole self—and his life to us. He calls us to do this in memory of him. We have taken this to mean we are to reenact the breaking of the bread and the sharing of the cup as an expression of our experience of his presence and gift of himself to us—and certainly it does mean that. But it means far more. We are called to do what he did, to be bread and wine as he is bread and wine, to be his body, to be his blood—to be self-givers and life-givers. We proclaim our willingness to answer his call with our "Amen" at the conclusion of the eucharistic prayer and at Communion as our individual response to "body of Christ" and "blood of Christ."

Let us look at bread now from our human experience. Bread begins with wheat. The wheat grows in the field and is harvested. It is crushed and ground into flour. The flour is mixed with liquid and other ingredients to become bound together, united, one. Then it is baked.

This process is a sign of how we grow within ourselves to become whole persons, as well as a sign of how a group of people develop as a family or a community. The one loaf is broken and shared—a sign of how, both as individuals and as family or community, we nourish each other, sharing our whole selves.

Our "Amen" means that we will become bread as Christ is bread; we will be his body. We will go through the process toward wholeness. We will share of ourselves, to nourish and be nourished.

Now let us consider wine from our human perspective. Wine begins with grapes. The grapes grow on the vine and are harvested. They are pressed and squeezed, giving up their juice. The juice is fermented—a long, slow process. Finally the juice becomes fine wine—quenching thirst, bringing warmth and joy and companionship—embodying a full, rich flavor with a certain tang which was not present in the juice at the beginning of the process.

The wine-making process is a sign of how our human life develops to its fullness, both as individuals and as community. The cup is shared—a sign of how we share with each other the richness and warmth and joy that is our life.

Our "Amen" means that we will become wine as Christ is wine; we will be his blood, his life. We will go through the process toward fullness of life, and we will share that life.

In the formation and sharing of both bread and wine, there are common elements. There is a growing time and a harvesting: a wrenching, violent separation from the parent stem. Then there is a grinding, a crushing, to bring forth the basic substances from which the bread and wine will be formed. There is a slowness, a time involved in the baking and in the fermentation. There is finally a completion, a coming together in wholeness. Then there seems to be another fragmentation when the bread is broken, as well as a diminishing when the bread and wine are consumed.

The gospels are full of experiences of Jesus which are reflected in the bread and wine formation processes. Generally, in the development of Jesus' ministry, he experienced a breaking away from some of the traditional beliefs and practices of Judaism. He must have felt some wrenching and pain in that process, as we do when we question and let go of some of our traditions, leaving behind the security of the "parent stem." He rejected much of the legalism of the traditional practices, but kept with him the valued beliefs—retaining much from the "parent plant," but transforming it. We do the same in our own growth process, as we form our personal values.

Throughout the gospels there are stories which manifest Jesus' strength and resilience in the face of the opposition of his enemies—much like a field of wheat in a strong wind. Jesus' sensitivity to the feelings of others is also shown repeatedly— reminiscent of the wheat responding to the gentlest breeze.

We, too, experience our own resiliency as well as our being battered by the storms of our lives. We experience our sensitivity as well as our insensitivity.

Jesus felt a crushing sadness as he grew in awareness and saw more and more clearly the inner as well as the outer pain and imprisonment of many, and the inability of some to see the hope and promise of his way. We feel similar emotions.

Jesus' final crushing feelings of betrayal came at the end of his life in his rejection by many of his own people, and even in his feeling of being abandoned by his Father, as he cried out from the cross. His essential strength and wholeness saw him through, however, to the final transformation in the resurrection.

Jesus' passion and death looked like a breaking and a diminishing, but this was only an illusion. What looked like death and failure was really a transformation to new life and victory. There became the possibility of ever greater sharing of life, no longer limited to the physical space and time of Jesus' historical life. This is reflected in the apparent breaking and diminishing of the bread and wine as a result of its sharing and being consumed. The bread is not destroyed; it is transformed to a new form of life as it nourishes the one who receives it. The wine is transformed also, now manifested in the less tangible but very real warmth and joy and fellowship expressed by those who receive it.

The breaking of the bread and the sharing of the cup are most deeply the sign of the death and resurrection of the Lord, and of our own daily dying and rising as we follow his way. Time after time, what is apparently destroyed is really transformed into new life.

In the words of St. Augustine in a fourth-century sermon: "If then you are the body of Christ and his members, it is your sacrament that reposes on the altar of the Lord. . . . Be what you see and receive what you are" (Sermon 272). "There you are on the table, and there you are in the chalice" (Sermon 229).

Meditation

Begin the meditation by partaking of a small piece of bread and a few sips of wine. This works well in a small group, where the bread would be broken and shared, and a single cup of wine would be shared. Feel the bread. Look at it. Smell it. Eat it slowly, savoring its texture and flavor. Do the same with the wine, savoring it fully. Experience the eating of the bread and the drinking of the wine as fully as possible. Then become quiet and relaxed.

Picture in your mind a field of golden wheat . . .
    ripe for the harvest.
    Imagine the sky . . . the clouds . . . the countryside.
    Breathe in the fragrances of the place.
    Feel the gentle breeze.
        See the waves of grain . . .
            as the wheat bends to and fro in the breeze.
    The breeze gradually becomes a strong wind.
        The wheat is bending to the ground . . .
            almost to the breaking point.
    And yet it springs back, recovers,
        stands tall again . . .
        as the wind subsides.

Imagine the field of wheat that is part of you . . .
    responding to the gentle breezes in your life,
        with sensitivity and awareness.
    Then a strong wind comes . . .
        and you are bent to the breaking point . . .
            and from somewhere deep within,
            there springs forth a strength,
            an ability to bounce back,
                to stand tall again.

Now move closer to the field,
    until you can touch the wheat.

Choose one stalk.
Look very closely at it.
Touch it.
Smell it.
Feel the small cluster of grain at the tip of the stalk,
    bulging with the promise of new life
        and growth and nourishment.
Imagine the grains of wheat that are part of you . . .
    ready for the harvest . . .
    containing the potential for new life . . .
        growth . . . nourishment . . .
        the capacity for moving life forward
            in the world that you touch . . .
        the ability to create.

Now the harvesters are ready.
    The grain is stripped from its stalk . . .
        taken to the mill . . .
        ground into flour . . .
        made ready for its task of
            giving and sharing life.
    Imagine your inner grains of wheat . . .
        being torn from your stalk . . .
            your roots . . .
            your security.
    Feel the violence of the grinding and crushing . . .
        the preparation for the giving and sharing of life.

Imagine yourself as the fine, rich flour,
    being bound together now
        as the warm liquid is mixed in . . .
        being reunited, made whole again . . . in a new way.

Now comes the kneading . . .
    back and forth . . .
        being pressed and released . . .

becoming elastic . . . resilient . . .
    like the stalks of wheat . . .
    and yet different . . . new.

Imagine how it feels to be the dough . . .
    becoming bound together . . . slowly . . .
        becoming elastic . . . resilient . . . expanding.

And then comes the baking, the final shaping . . .
    the end of the bread making and
        the beginning of the life-giving . . .
            the life-sharing.

Now picture in your mind a vineyard.
    Imagine the surrounding countryside, the sky.
        Go closer and see the grapes . . .
            hanging heavy on the vines . . .
            ripe for the harvest . . .
            swollen with the promise of nourishment
            and refreshment.
    Imagine the harvesting . . .
        the grapes being plucked from their vines,
            carried to the wine maker,
                to the wine press . . .
            and then crushed . . .
                yielding up their rich juices . . .
            and then the fermentation . . .
                the long, slow process of transformation.

Imagine the vineyard that is part of you . . .
    the grapes being plucked away from your vine . . .
        your roots . . .
            your security.
    Feel the crushing . . . the pressing of the grapes . . .
        yielding forth the life-giving juices . . .
    and then the long, slow transformation . . .

the living process of fermentation . . .
    growing richer and deeper in flavor . . .
    gaining in capacity for joy and warmth,
        for intoxication with life . . .
    gaining also a tang, a poignancy, a depth.

Then there is the coming to completion . . .
    becoming wine . . .
        and the readiness for sharing.

Now . . . the bread of your self and
    the cup of your life are shared . . .
        bringing joy . . .
            spreading warmth . . .
                drawing together in fellowship . . .
                    nourishing life . . . quenching thirst . . .
                creating anew.

And so we are bread . . .
    and we are wine . . .
        the body of Christ . . .
            the blood of Christ . . .
                dying and rising again and again . . .
    and we dare to answer . . .
    we rejoice to answer . . .
            AMEN

Now eat the bread and drink the wine again, slowly and reverently. Taste your own bread-ness and your own wine-ness, united with the bread-ness and the wine-ness of the risen Lord. Call to mind your family and your community, and how together you are like bread and like wine . . .
    as all become more and more fully
        the body of Christ, the blood of Christ . . .
            as we die and rise with him . . .
                as we share ourselves, as we share our lives.

7

THE HEALER

We will conclude our exploration of the inner meaning of the gospels with a consideration of the familiar parable of the Good Samaritan, Luke 10:25–37. As you read the passage, pause at each asterisk and imagine the feelings of the character just introduced in the story. There is the robbed and wounded traveler, the priest and Levite (considered as one figure), and the Samaritan. It might be helpful to write down the emotions you think are being experienced by each.

Then a certain teacher of the Law came up and tried to trap Jesus. "Teacher," he asked, "what must I do to receive eternal life?" Jesus answered him, "What do the Scriptures say? How do you interpret them?" The man answered: " 'You must love the Lord your God with all your heart, and with all your soul, and with all your strength, and with all your mind'; and, 'You must love your neighbor as yourself.' " "Your answer is correct," replied Jesus; "do this and you will live."

But the teacher of the Law wanted to put himself in the right, so he asked Jesus, "Who is my neighbor?" Jesus answered: "A certain man was going down from Jerusalem to Jericho, when robbers attacked him, stripped him and beat him up, leaving him half dead.*

It so happened that a priest was going down that road; when he saw the man he walked on by, on the other side. In the same way a Levite also came there, went over and looked at the man, and then walked on by, the other side.* But a certain Samaritan who was traveling that way came upon him, and when he saw the man his heart was filled with pity.* He went over to him, poured oil and wine on his wounds and bandaged them; then he put the man on his own animal and took him to an inn, where he took care of him. The next day he took out two silver coins and gave them to the innkeeper. 'Take care of him,' he told the innkeeper, 'and when I come back this way I will pay you back whatever you spend on him.' " And Jesus concluded, "Which one of these three seems to you to have been a neighbor to the man attacked by the robbers?" The teacher of the Law answered, "The one who was kind to him." Jesus replied, "You go, then, and do the same." (Good News Bible)

Step 1—Scriptural Background

Jesus' Jewish audience would notice an unusual attitude revealed by Jesus in the story. The priest and Levite, being leaders in the Jewish religion, would be expected to be models of behavior. The Samaritans, on the other hand, were looked down upon because of their unorthodox beliefs. This is one of many incidents in which Jesus challenges the narrow thinking of some of the Jews.

Step 2—Re-creating the Event

Imagine the scene of the story. The road from Jerusalem to Jericho is desolate and rocky. Robbers often lurked in the area, waiting to attack unprotected travelers.

How do you think the traveler feels as he lies by the side of the road, beaten and half dead? Hurting? In great pain? Afraid? Abandoned? Helpless? Foolish (for traveling without more protection)? Angry? Weak? Robbed/cheated?

What emotions do you think the priest/Levite experiences while passing by? Disgust? Fear? Revulsion? Superiority?

How do you think the Samaritan feels as he sees the injured traveler and begins to care for him? Torn at first, remembering the business to which he must attend? Compassionate?

Step 3—Inner Meaning

Considering the feelings of the injured traveler, try to identify any corresponding emotions within yourself—the part of yourself that feels hurt, robbed, abandoned. Then look for your inner priest/Levite—a part of yourself that looks with disgust or superiority upon your hurting self, and is unwilling to expend any effort toward healing. Now try to find your inner Good Samaritan—a strong and able and compassionate part of yourself that can heal your inner wounds.

Let us not forget about our inner robbers, for they have inflicted the wounds and robbed us of our valuables in the first place. One good clue to identifying our robbers is that they use the words "should" and "ought" very frequently. They strip us of our value as a person, rob us of our self-esteem, and inflict painful wounds in the process.

Step 4—Meditation

Become quiet and relaxed, closing your eyes and breathing slowly and gently. Allow the story to unfold in your imagination, experiencing the robbers, the traveler, the priest/Levite, and the Samaritan as parts of yourself. All the action takes place within yourself. You may want to speak to one or all of the characters, or write out a dialogue. If you feel so inclined, let the story progress beyond the passage itself, perhaps experiencing the continuing care of the traveler by the innkeeper or the return of the Samaritan.

The story of the Good Samaritan can be seen as a model of human growth and wholeness, with the Samaritan symbolizing the healing power and presence of Christ within each of us.

Notice the portion of the story taken by each character. The robbers have only a half of one sentence. The priest and Levite have only one sentence each. The major part of the story concerns the healing and care of the traveler by the Samaritan. Human growth does often involve our own attacks on our self-esteem, robbing ourselves of our personal value—as well as disgust with ourselves and a refusal to attend to our wounds. For greater wholeness, though, the main portion of our energy and attention is best spent on the regaining of our self-esteem, and involves our nurturing our own sense of compassion toward ourselves. Lack of caring for ourselves is likely to be reflected outward in an inability to feel compassion toward others.

In a group meditation which I led using this parable, the participants experienced the story in very individual ways. One person's Samaritan was very tiny, about one inch tall, while another could not imagine her Samaritan at all. Another person's priest/Levite stayed in the way, so that her Samaritan could not get to her injured self. One person dwelt on the continuing care of the innkeeper, while another experienced the soothing washing and binding of the wounds by her Samaritan at the inn.

When we compare our meditation with the scriptural story, we can gain a valuable insight concerning an area in which we may be ready for growth. For example, the person whose priest/Levite were in the way of her Samaritan might pay attention to ways in which she thinks she does not deserve care or perhaps in which her own woundedness seems unimportant. She may wish to concentrate on sending these attitudes on "down the road" and focus her attention on tending to her own healing. She may need to convince herself that she deserves this care and attention.

It can be fruitful to return to the parable of the Good Samaritan occasionally in meditation. We are likely to experience the story differently each time we use it. Our meditation experience can point the way to the part of ourselves that most needs our attention at the moment. It could call our attention to a need for healing as well as to a barrier to that healing.

If you wish to use this approach to the gospels for other passages that we have not explored, the following suggestions may be helpful:

1. Choose passages which involve interaction among the characters.
2. Focus on the emotions of each figure in the story.
3. Seek the inner meaning of the story for yourself by trying to identify similar emotions in your own experience at the present time. Ask how certain figures in the passage are like a part of yourself.
4. In meditation, try the following:
   a. Allow the story to unfold in your imagination, simply observing it. Let it go beyond the end of the actual scripture passage if desired.
   b. Interrupt the story if you wish, and initiate a dialogue with one or more of the figures. This can be done in writing if that is helpful.
   c. Call on Jesus for guidance, comfort, strength, or simply to be present with you.

Using the passage as a model for wholeness and balance, compare your meditation with it. Observe how it differs and try to see if it offers an insight to a way of growth that would be appropriate for you at the present time. However, avoid trying too hard to find a definite interpretation of a meditation. If you relax and just let it be, and cherish it, you are more likely to gain insights from it. Recording your meditations in a journal for both present and future reflection can be helpful. Keep in mind that a meditation of this type is symbolic and uses the language of imagery. To attempt to convert it to words and logical thought processes tends to cloud the meaning rather than clarify it.

As you continue to plumb your own depths through meditation and to draw to consciousness your inner resources, you will become more and more adept at understanding yourself and where best to focus your energy and attention as you travel through life. You will have a more complete awareness of your own growth as you perceive your life not only through rational thinking, but also through the imagery and symbolism of your inner self. You will find that you can see yourself and others more and more clearly, love more deeply and with greater compassion, and live your life more fully. You will come to know your God within ever more intimately.

May it be our vision and our dream that,
    hand in hand with our risen Lord,
        we may drink deeply of the cup of life,
            savoring its flavor,
                relishing its aroma,
                    absorbing its lights and its shadows,
        and may we be filled to our depths
            with life's beauty,
                its poignancy,
                    its richness,
                        its mystery,
                            its divinity.